ITALIAN
SLOW COOKING

Publications International, Ltd.

Pictured on the front cover: Meatballs and Spaghetti Sauce *(page 116).*

Pictured on the back cover *(counterclockwise):* Italian Wedding Soup with Three-Cheese Tortellini *(page 54),* Chicken Vesuvio *(page 80),* Cheesy Polenta *(page 176)* and Beans and Spinach Bruschetta *(page 24).*

CONTENTS

SEAFOOD CIOPPINO P. 44

SLOW COOKING TIPS

SIZES OF **CROCK-POT®** SLOW COOKERS

Smaller **CROCK-POT®** slow cookers—such as 1- to 3½-quart models—are the perfect size for cooking for singles, a couple or empty nesters (and also for serving dips).

While medium-size **CROCK-POT®** slow cookers (those holding somewhere between 3 quarts and 5 quarts) will easily cook enough food at one time to feed a small family, they are also convenient for holiday side dishes or appetizers.

Large **CROCK-POT®** slow cookers are great for large family dinners, holiday entertaining and potluck suppers. A 6- to 7-quart model is ideal if you like to make meals in advance. Or, have dinner tonight and store leftovers for later.

TYPES OF **CROCK-POT®** SLOW COOKERS

Current **CROCK-POT®** slow cookers come equipped with many different features and benefits, from auto cook programs to oven-safe stoneware to timed programming. Please visit **WWW.CROCK-POT.COM** to find the **CROCK-POT®** slow cooker that best suits your needs.

How you plan to use a **CROCK-POT®** slow cooker may affect the model you choose to purchase. For everyday cooking, choose a size large enough to serve your family. If you plan to use the **CROCK-POT®** slow cooker primarily for entertaining, choose one of the larger sizes. Basic **CROCK-POT®** slow cookers can hold as little as 16 ounces or as much as 7 quarts. The smallest sizes are great for keeping dips warm on a buffet, while the larger sizes can more readily fit large quantities of food and larger roasts.

COOKING, STIRRING AND FOOD SAFETY

CROCK-POT® slow cookers are safe to leave unattended. The outer heating base may get hot as it cooks, but it should not pose a fire hazard. The heating element in the heating base functions at a low wattage and is safe for your countertops.

Your **CROCK-POT®** slow cooker should be filled about one-half to three-fourths full for most recipes unless otherwise instructed. Lean meats such as chicken or pork tenderloin will cook faster than meats with more connective tissue and fat such as beef chuck or pork shoulder. Bone-in meats will take longer than boneless cuts. Typical **CROCK-POT®** slow cooker dishes take approximately 7 to 8 hours to reach the simmer point on LOW and about 3 to 4 hours on HIGH. Once the vegetables and meat start to simmer and braise, their flavors will fully blend and meat will become fall-off-the-bone tender.

According to the U.S. Department of Agriculture, all bacteria are killed at a temperature of 165°F. It's important to follow the recommended cooking times and not to open the lid often, especially early in the cooking process when heat is building up inside the unit. If you need to open the lid to check on your food or are adding additional ingredients, remember to allow additional cooking time if necessary to ensure food is cooked through and tender.

Large **CROCK-POT®** slow cookers, the 6- to 7-quart sizes, may benefit from a quick stir halfway through cook time to help distribute heat and promote even cooking. It's usually unnecessary to stir at all, as even ½ cup liquid will help to distribute heat, and the stoneware is the perfect medium for holding food at an even temperature throughout the cooking process.

OVEN-SAFE STONEWARE

All **CROCK-POT®** slow cooker removable stoneware inserts may (without their lids) be used safely in ovens at up to 400°F. In addition, all **CROCK-POT®** slow cookers are microwavable without their lids. If you own another slow cooker brand, please refer to your owner's manual for specific stoneware cooking medium tolerances.

FROZEN FOOD

Frozen food can be successfully cooked in a **CROCK-POT®** slow cooker. However, it will require longer cooking time than the same recipe made with fresh food. Using an instant-read thermometer is recommended to ensure meat is fully cooked.

PASTA AND RICE

If you are converting a recipe for your **CROCK-POT®** slow cooker that calls for uncooked pasta, first cook the pasta on the stovetop just until slightly tender. Then add the pasta to the **CROCK-POT®** slow cooker.

If you are converting a recipe for the **CROCK-POT®** slow cooker that calls for cooked rice, stir in raw rice with the other recipe ingredients plus ¼ cup extra liquid per ¼ cup of raw rice.

ASIAGO AND ASPARAGUS
RISOTTO-STYLE RICE P. 168

BEANS

Beans must be softened completely before combining with sugar and/or acidic foods in the **CROCK-POT®** slow cooker. Sugar and acid have a hardening effect on beans and will prevent softening. Fully cooked canned beans may be used as a substitute for dried beans.

VEGETABLES

Root vegetables often cook more slowly than meat. Cut vegetables accordingly to cook at the same rate as meat—large or small or lean versus marbled—and place near the sides or bottom of the stoneware to facilitate cooking.

HERBS

Fresh herbs add flavor and color when added at the end of the cooking cycle; if added at the beginning, many fresh herbs' flavor will dissipate over long cook times. Ground and/or dried herbs and spices work well in slow cooking and may be added at the beginning of cook time. For dishes with shorter cook times, hearty fresh herbs such as rosemary and thyme hold up well. The flavor power of all herbs and spices can vary greatly depending on their particular strength and shelf life. Use chili powders and garlic powder sparingly, as these can sometimes intensify over the long cook times. Always taste the finished dish and correct seasonings including salt and pepper.

LIQUIDS

It is not necessary to use more than ½ to 1 cup liquid in most instances. Most juices in meats and vegetables are retained more in slow cooking than in conventional cooking. Excess liquid can be cooked down and concentrated after slow cooking, either on the stovetop or by removing the meat and vegetables from the stoneware. Then stirring in one of the following thickeners and setting the **CROCK-POT®** slow cooker to HIGH. Cover and cook the liquid on HIGH for approximately 15 minutes or until thickened.

FLOUR: All-purpose flour is often used to thicken soups or stews. Stir water into the flour in a small bowl until smooth. With the **CROCK-POT®** slow cooker on HIGH, whisk flour mixture into the liquid in the **CROCK-POT®** slow cooker. Cover; cook on HIGH 15 minutes or until the mixture is thickened.

CORNSTARCH: Cornstarch gives sauces a clear, shiny appearance; it's used most often for sweet dessert sauces and stir-fry sauces. Stir water into the cornstarch in a small bowl until the cornstarch is dissolved. Quickly stir this mixture into the liquid in the **CROCK-POT®** slow cooker; the sauce will thicken as soon as the liquid simmers. Cornstarch breaks down with too much heat, so never add it at the beginning of the slow cooking process and turn off the heat as soon as the sauce thickens.

MILK

Milk, cream and sour cream break down during extended cooking. When possible, add them during the last 15 to 30 minutes of slow cooking, until just heated through. Condensed soups may be substituted for milk and may cook for extended times.

FISH

Fish is delicate and should be stirred into the **CROCK-POT®** slow cooker gently during the last 15 to 30 minutes of cooking. Cover; cook just until cooked through and serve immediately.

BAKED GOODS

If you wish to prepare bread, cakes or pudding cakes in a **CROCK-POT®** slow cooker, you may want to purchase a covered, vented metal cake pan accessory for your **CROCK-POT®** slow cooker. You can also use any straight-sided soufflé dish or deep cake pan that will fit into the stoneware of your unit. Baked goods can be prepared directly in the stoneware; however, they can be a little difficult to remove from the insert, so follow the recipe directions carefully.

ANTIPASTI FAVORITES

CAPONATA

Makes about 5 cups

1 medium eggplant (about 1 pound), peeled and cut into ½-inch pieces

1 can (about 14 ounces) diced tomatoes

1 medium onion, chopped

1 red bell pepper, cut into ½-inch pieces

½ cup medium salsa

¼ cup extra virgin olive oil

2 tablespoons capers, drained

2 tablespoons balsamic vinegar

3 cloves garlic, minced

1 teaspoon dried oregano

⅓ cup packed fresh basil, cut into thin strips

2 loaves (24 slices) Italian or French bread, sliced and toasted

1. Combine eggplant, tomatoes, onion, bell pepper, salsa, oil, capers, vinegar, garlic and oregano in **CROCK-POT®** slow cooker; stir to blend. Cover; cook on LOW 7 to 8 hours.

2. Stir in basil. Serve at room temperature with toasted bread.

COCKTAIL MEATBALLS

Makes about 24 meatballs

1 pound ground beef

1 pound bulk pork or Italian sausage

1 cup cracker crumbs

1 cup finely chopped onion

1 cup finely chopped green bell pepper

½ cup milk

1 egg, beaten

2 teaspoons salt

1 teaspoon Italian seasoning

¼ teaspoon black pepper

1 cup ketchup

¾ cup packed dark brown sugar

½ cup (1 stick) butter

½ cup cider vinegar

¼ cup lemon juice

¼ cup water

1 teaspoon yellow mustard

¼ teaspoon garlic salt

1. Preheat oven to 350°F. Combine beef, pork, cracker crumbs, onion, bell pepper, milk, egg, salt, Italian seasoning and black pepper in large bowl; mix well. Form beef mixture into 24 (1-inch) meatballs. Place meatballs onto two nonstick baking sheets. Bake 25 minutes or until browned.

2. Meanwhile, place ketchup, brown sugar, butter, vinegar, lemon juice, water, mustard and garlic salt into **CROCK-POT®** slow cooker; stir to blend. Cover; cook on HIGH 15 to 20 minutes or until heated through.

3. Turn **CROCK-POT®** slow cooker to LOW. Remove meatballs to **CROCK-POT®** slow cooker; toss to coat. Cover; cook on LOW 2 hours.

SPICY ITALIAN BEEF

Makes 8 to 10 servings

1   boneless beef chuck roast
    (3 to 4 pounds)*

1   jar (12 ounces) pepperoncini
    peppers**

1   can (about 14 ounces) beef broth

1   can (12 ounces) beer

1   onion, minced

2   tablespoons Italian seasoning

1   loaf French bread, cut into thick
    slices

8   to 10 slices provolone cheese
    (optional)

*Unless you have a 5-, 6- or 7-quart **CROCK-POT®**
slow cooker, cut any roast larger than 2½ pounds
in half so it cooks completely.

**Pepperoncini peppers are pickled peppers sold in
jars with brine. They are available in the condiment
aisle of large supermarkets.

1. Place roast in **CROCK-POT®** slow cooker. Drain peppers. Pull off stem ends and discard. Add peppers, broth, beer, onion and Italian seasoning to **CROCK-POT®** slow cooker; do not stir. Cover; cook on LOW 8 to 10 hours.

2. Remove beef to large cutting board; shred with two forks. Return beef to cooking liquid; mix well. Serve on French bread. Top with cheese, if desired.

SUN-DRIED TOMATO APPETIZER SPREAD

Makes 3 cups

3 cups chopped onion

3 jars (about 7 ounces *each*) sun-dried tomatoes, packed in oil, drained and finely chopped

½ cup red wine vinegar

3 tablespoons sugar

1 tablespoon minced garlic

1 piece (2 inches) fresh ginger, peeled and grated

1 teaspoon herbes de Provence

½ teaspoon salt

1 package (8 ounces) cream cheese

Sprigs fresh basil (optional)

Assorted crackers

1. Combine onion, sun-dried tomatoes, vinegar, sugar, garlic, ginger, herbes de Provence and salt in 2-quart **CROCK-POT®** slow cooker; stir gently to mix. Cover; cook on LOW 4 to 5 hours or on HIGH 3 hours, stirring occasionally. Let mixture cool before using.

2. To serve, slice cream cheese in half horizontally (use dental floss for clean cut) and separate pieces. Spread ⅓ cup tomato mixture onto 1 cream cheese half. Top with remaining cream cheese half and spread ⅓ cup tomato mixture on top. Garnish with fresh basil sprigs and serve with crackers. Refrigerate or freeze remaining tomato mixture for another use.

FOCACCIA WITH ROSEMARY AND ROMANO

Makes 8 to 10 servings

1¼ cups warm water (100° to 110°F)

1 packet (¼ ounce) active dry yeast

1 tablespoon sugar

3 to 3½ cups all-purpose flour

1½ tablespoons finely chopped fresh rosemary

2 teaspoons salt

½ teaspoon red pepper flakes

3 tablespoons extra virgin olive oil

¼ cup grated Romano cheese

1. Coat inside of **CROCK-POT®** slow cooker with nonstick cooking spray. Combine water, yeast and sugar in small bowl; let stand 5 minutes until frothy. Combine flour, rosemary, salt and red pepper flakes in large bowl; stir to blend. Pour water mixture and oil into flour mixture; stir until soft dough forms. Turn dough out onto lightly floured surface; knead 5 minutes. Place dough in **CROCK-POT®** slow cooker; stretch to fit bottom. Cover; let stand 1 hour in warm place (85°F) until doubled in bulk.

2. Gently press dough with fingertips to deflate. Sprinkle with cheese. Cover; let rise 30 minutes. Place clean, dry towel over top of **CROCK-POT®** slow cooker; then replace the lid. Cover; cook on HIGH 2 hours or until dough is lightly browned on sides. Remove to wire rack. Let stand 10 to 15 minutes before slicing.

WARM BLUE CRAB BRUSCHETTA

Makes 16 servings

4 cups peeled, seeded and diced plum tomatoes

1 cup diced white onion

⅓ cup olive oil

2 tablespoons sugar

2 tablespoons balsamic vinegar

2 teaspoons minced garlic

½ teaspoon dried oregano

1 pound lump blue crabmeat, picked over for shells

1½ teaspoons kosher salt

½ teaspoon cracked black pepper

⅓ cup minced fresh basil

2 baguettes, sliced and toasted

1. Combine tomatoes, onion, oil, sugar, vinegar, garlic and oregano in **CROCK-POT®** slow cooker; stir to blend. Cover; cook on LOW 2 hours.

2. Stir crabmeat, salt and pepper into **CROCK-POT®** slow cooker, taking care not to break up crabmeat. Cover; cook on LOW 1 hour. Fold in basil. Serve on toasted baguette slices.

SERVING SUGGESTION: Crab topping can also be served on Melba toast or whole grain crackers.

BAGNA CAUDA

Makes 1⅓ cups

¾ cup olive oil

6 tablespoons butter, softened

12 anchovy fillets, drained

6 cloves garlic

⅛ teaspoon red pepper flakes

Optional dippers: sugar snap peas, bell pepper slices, green onions, cucumber spears, zucchini spears, carrot sticks and/or bread sticks

1. Place oil, butter, anchovies, garlic and red pepper flakes in food processor or blender; process 30 seconds or until smooth. Heat medium saucepan over medium heat. Pour oil mixture into saucepan; bring to a boil. Reduce heat to medium low; simmer 5 minutes.

2. Coat inside of **CROCK-POT®** "No-Dial" slow cooker with nonstick cooking spray. Fill with warm dip. Serve with dippers as desired.

BEANS AND SPINACH BRUSCHETTA

Makes 16 servings

2 cans (about 15 ounces *each*) Great Northern or cannellini beans, rinsed and drained

3 cloves garlic, minced

Salt and black pepper

6 cups spinach, loosely packed and finely chopped

1 tablespoon red wine vinegar

16 slices whole grain baguette

2 tablespoons extra virgin olive oil

1. Combine beans, garlic, salt and black pepper in **CROCK-POT®** slow cooker; stir to blend. Cover; cook on LOW 3 hours or until beans are tender. Turn off heat. Mash beans with potato masher. Stir in spinach and vinegar.

2. Preheat grill or broiler. Brush baguette slices with oil. Grill 5 to 7 minutes or until bread is golden brown and crisp. Top with bean mixture and spinach.

MINI MEATBALL GRINDERS

Makes 12 servings

1 can (about 14 ounces) diced tomatoes, drained and juices reserved

1 can (8 ounces) tomato sauce

¼ cup chopped onion

2 tablespoons tomato paste

1 teaspoon Italian seasoning

1 pound ground chicken

½ cup fresh whole wheat or white bread crumbs (1 slice bread)

1 egg white, lightly beaten

3 tablespoons finely chopped fresh Italian parsley

2 cloves garlic, minced

¼ teaspoon salt

⅛ teaspoon black pepper

Nonstick cooking spray

4 hard rolls, split and toasted

3 tablespoons grated Parmesan cheese (optional)

1. Combine tomatoes, ½ cup reserved juice, tomato sauce, onion, tomato paste and Italian seasoning in **CROCK-POT®** slow cooker. Cover; cook on LOW 3 to 4 hours.

2. Prepare meatballs halfway through cooking time. Combine chicken, bread crumbs, egg white, parsley, garlic, salt and pepper in medium bowl; mix well. Shape mixture into 12 meatballs. Cover; refrigerate 30 minutes.

3. Spray medium skillet with cooking spray; heat over medium heat. Add meatballs; cook 8 to 10 minutes or until well browned on all sides. Remove meatballs to **CROCK-POT®** slow cooker using slotted spoon. Cover; cook on LOW 1 to 2 hours or until no longer pink in center.

4. Place 3 meatballs in each roll; top with sauce. Sprinkle with cheese, if desired. Cut each roll into thirds.

CHICKEN AND ASIAGO STUFFED MUSHROOMS

Makes 4 to 5 servings

20 large white mushrooms, stems removed and reserved

3 tablespoons extra virgin olive oil, divided

¼ cup finely chopped onion

2 cloves garlic, minced

¼ cup Madeira wine

½ pound chicken sausage, casings removed or ground chicken

1 cup grated Asiago cheese

¼ cup Italian-style seasoned dry bread crumbs

3 tablespoons chopped fresh Italian parsley

½ teaspoon salt

¼ teaspoon black pepper

1. Lightly brush mushroom caps with 1 tablespoon oil; set aside. Finely chop mushroom stems.

2. Heat remaining 2 tablespoons oil in large skillet over medium-high heat. Add onion; cook 1 minute or until just beginning to soften. Add mushroom stems; cook 5 to 6 minutes or until beginning to brown. Stir in garlic; cook 1 minute.

3. Pour in wine; cook 1 minute. Add sausage; cook 3 to 4 minutes or until no longer pink, stirring to break into small pieces. Remove from heat; cool 5 minutes. Stir in cheese, bread crumbs, parsley, salt and pepper.

4. Divide mushroom-sausage mixture among mushroom caps, pressing slightly to compress. Place stuffed mushroom caps in single layer in **CROCK-POT®** slow cooker. Cover; cook on LOW 4 hours or on HIGH 2 hours.

TIP: Stuffed mushrooms are a great way to impress guests with your gourmet cooking skills. These appetizers appear time intensive and fancy, but they are actually simple with the help of a **CROCK-POT®** slow cooker.

TOMATO TOPPING FOR BRUSCHETTA

Makes 8 servings

6 medium tomatoes, peeled, seeded and diced

2 stalks celery, chopped

2 shallots, chopped

4 pepperoncini peppers, chopped*

2 tablespoons olive oil

2 teaspoons tomato paste

1 teaspoon salt

½ teaspoon black pepper

8 slices country bread or other large round bread

2 cloves garlic, crushed

*Pepperoncini are pickled peppers sold in jars with brine. They are available in the condiment aisle of large supermarkets.

1. Drain tomatoes in fine-mesh strainer. Combine tomatoes, celery, shallots, pepperoncini peppers, oil, tomato paste, salt and black pepper in **CROCK-POT®** slow cooker; stir gently to blend. Cover; cook on LOW 45 minutes to 1 hour.

2. Toast bread; immediately rub with garlic. Spread tomato topping on bread to serve.

VARIATION: To serve as a main dish, omit bread and garlic and toss tomato topping with cooked penne pasta. You may also spoon the topping over roasted chicken breasts as a flavorful sauce.

LEMON AND GARLIC SHRIMP

Makes 6 to 8 servings

1 pound large raw shrimp, peeled and deveined (with tails on)

½ cup (1 stick) unsalted butter, cubed

3 cloves garlic, crushed

2 tablespoons lemon juice

½ teaspoon paprika

Salt and black pepper

2 tablespoons finely chopped fresh Italian parsley

Crusty bread, sliced (optional)

1. Coat inside of **CROCK-POT®** slow cooker with nonstick cooking spray. Add shrimp, butter and garlic; mix well. Cover; cook on HIGH 1¼ hours.

2. Turn off heat. Stir in lemon juice, paprika, salt and pepper. Spoon shrimp and liquid into large serving bowl. Sprinkle with parsley. Serve with crusty bread for dipping, if desired.

PEPPERONI PIZZA

Makes 12 servings

1 package (about 3 ounces) pepperoni, divided

1 teaspoon minced garlic

¼ teaspoon red pepper flakes

1 package (about 16 ounces) refrigerated biscuits, each biscuit cut into 6 pieces

1 can (15 ounces) pizza sauce

1 small green bell pepper, chopped

1 small yellow bell pepper, chopped

1 package (8 ounces) shredded mozzarella cheese

1. Coat inside of **CROCK-POT®** slow cooker with nonstick cooking spray. Prepare foil handles by tearing off four 18×2-inch strips heavy foil (or use regular foil folded to double thickness). Crisscross foil strips in spoke design; place in round **CROCK-POT®** slow cooker. Spray foil handles with cooking spray.

2. Chop half of pepperoni slices. Combine chopped pepperoni, garlic and red pepper flakes in medium bowl. Roll each biscuit piece into pepperoni mixture; place in **CROCK-POT®** slow cooker. Pour half of pizza sauce over dough. Reserve remaining pizza sauce. Top sauce with bell peppers, mozzarella cheese and remaining half of pepperoni slices.

3. Cover; cook on LOW 3 hours. Turn off heat. Let pizza stand 10 to 15 minutes. Remove from **CROCK-POT®** slow cooker using foil handles. Serve with remaining pizza sauce for dipping, if desired.

SOUPS & STEWS

CHICKEN ORZO SOUP

Makes 6 to 8 servings

1 tablespoon vegetable oil

1 onion, diced

1 fennel bulb, quartered, cored, thinly sliced, tops removed and fronds reserved for garnish

2 teaspoons minced garlic

8 cups chicken broth

2 boneless, skinless chicken breasts (8 ounces *each*)

2 carrots, peeled and thinly sliced

2 sprigs fresh thyme

1 whole bay leaf

Salt and black pepper

½ cup uncooked orzo

1. Heat oil in large skillet over medium heat. Add onion and fennel bulb; cook 8 minutes or until tender. Add garlic; cook and stir 1 minute. Remove to **CROCK-POT®** slow cooker. Add broth, chicken, carrots, thyme, bay leaf, salt and pepper. Cover; cook on HIGH 2 to 3 hours.

2. Remove chicken to large cutting board; shred with two forks. Add orzo to **CROCK-POT®** slow cooker. Cover; cook on HIGH 30 minutes. Stir shredded chicken back into **CROCK-POT®** slow cooker. Remove and discard thyme sprigs and bay leaf. Garnish each serving with fennel fronds.

PENNE PASTA ZUPPA

Makes 6 servings

1 can (about 15 ounces) cannellini beans, rinsed and drained

2 medium yellow squash, diced

2 ripe tomatoes, diced

2 small red potatoes, cubed

2 leeks, sliced lengthwise into quarters then chopped

1 carrot, diced

¼ pound fresh green beans, washed, stemmed and diced

2 fresh sage leaves, minced

1 teaspoon salt

½ teaspoon black pepper

8 cups water

¼ pound uncooked penne pasta

Grated Romano cheese (optional)

1. Combine beans, squash, tomatoes, potatoes, leeks, carrot, green beans, sage, salt and pepper in **CROCK-POT**® slow cooker. Add water; stir well to combine. Cover; cook on LOW 8 hours, stirring halfway through cooking time.

2. Turn **CROCK-POT**® slow cooker to HIGH. Add pasta. Cover; cook on HIGH 30 minutes or until pasta is cooked through. Garnish with cheese.

NANA'S MINI MEATBALL SOUP

Makes 6 to 8 servings

1   **pound ground beef**

1   **pound ground pork**

1½   **cups finely grated Pecorino Romano or Parmesan cheese**

1   **cup seasoned dry bread crumbs**

2   **eggs**

1   **bunch fresh Italian parsley**

Salt and black pepper

3   **quarts chicken broth**

1   **bunch escarole, coarsely chopped***

½   **(16-ounce) package ditalini pasta, cooked and drained**

*You may substitute spinach.

1. Combine beef, pork, cheese, bread crumbs, eggs, parsley, salt and pepper in large bowl until well blended. Shape into ¾-inch meatballs.

2. Add meatballs and broth to **CROCK-POT®** slow cooker. Cover; cook on LOW 9 hours or on HIGH 5 hours.

3. Add escarole. Cover; cook on LOW 15 minutes or until wilted. Stir in pasta just before serving.

TUSCAN BEAN AND PROSCIUTTO SOUP

Makes 6 servings

2 tablespoons unsalted butter

4 slices prosciutto*

3 cups water

1 cup dried navy beans, rinsed and sorted

½ cup dried lima beans, rinsed and sorted

1 medium yellow onion, finely chopped

1 tablespoon chopped fresh cilantro

1 teaspoon salt

1 teaspoon ground cumin

1 teaspoon black pepper

½ teaspoon ground paprika

2 cans (15 ounces *each*) diced tomatoes

Substitute 4 slices bacon, if desired.

1. Melt butter in large skillet over medium-high heat. Add prosciutto; cook until crisp. Remove to paper towels to cool.

2. Crumble prosciutto into small pieces in **CROCK-POT®** slow cooker. Add water, beans, onion, cilantro, salt, cumin, pepper and paprika; stir to blend. Cover; cook on LOW 10 to 12 hours.

3. Add tomatoes; stir until well blended. Turn **CROCK-POT®** slow cooker to HIGH. Cover; cook on HIGH 30 to 40 minutes or until soup is heated through.

SEAFOOD CIOPPINO

Makes 4 servings

1 tablespoon olive oil

1 medium fennel bulb, thinly sliced

1 medium onion, chopped

4 cloves garlic, minced

1 teaspoon dried basil

¼ teaspoon saffron threads, crushed (optional)

1 can (about 14 ounces) diced tomatoes

1 bottle (8 ounces) clam juice

16 little neck clams, scrubbed

24 mussels, scrubbed

1 pound cod fillet, cut into 8 pieces

8 ounces large raw shrimp, peeled and deveined (with tails on)

½ teaspoon salt

⅛ teaspoon black pepper

1. Coat inside of **CROCK-POT®** slow cooker with nonstick cooking spray. Heat oil in large skillet over medium-high heat. Add fennel, onion, garlic, basil and saffron, if desired; cook and stir 4 to 5 minutes or until vegetables are softened. Remove onion mixture to **CROCK-POT®** slow cooker. Stir in tomatoes and clam juice.

2. Cover; cook on HIGH 2 to 3 hours. Add clams. Cover; cook on HIGH 30 minutes. Add mussels. Cover; cook on HIGH 15 minutes.

3. Season cod and shrimp with salt and pepper. Place on top of shellfish. Cover; cook on HIGH 25 to 30 minutes until clams and mussels have opened and fish is cooked through. Discard any unopened clams or mussels.

TUSCAN BEEF STEW

Makes 6 to 8 servings

½ cup hot beef broth

¼ cup dried porcini mushrooms

2 pounds cubed beef stew meat
Salt and black pepper

1 tablespoon olive oil

3 slices bacon, diced and crisp-cooked

3 cups assorted mushrooms (such as portobello, shiitake or cremini), sliced

1 can (about 14 ounces) diced tomatoes with roasted garlic

1 cup frozen pearl onions, thawed

1 cup baby carrots, cut into ½-inch pieces

1 cup dry red wine

¼ cup tomato paste

1 tablespoon chopped fresh rosemary *or* 1 teaspoon dried rosemary

½ teaspoon sugar

2 tablespoons all-purpose flour

2 tablespoons butter, softened
Hot cooked pasta

1. Combine broth and dried mushrooms in small bowl; let stand 20 to 25 minutes or until softened. Remove mushrooms from broth; coarsely chop. Reserve broth.

2. Season beef with salt and pepper. Heat oil in large skillet over medium-high heat. Add beef; cook and stir 6 to 8 minutes or until browned on all sides. Remove to **CROCK-POT®** slow cooker.

3. Add bacon, chopped porcini mushrooms, sliced mushrooms, tomatoes, onions, carrots, wine, tomato paste, rosemary and sugar to **CROCK-POT®** slow cooker. Carefully pour reserved beef broth over top, being sure to keep sediment in bottom of bowl. Cover; cook on LOW 7 to 8 hours.

4. Combine flour and butter in small bowl; mash into smooth paste. Stir half of paste into cooking liquid. Cover; cook on LOW 15 minutes. If thicker gravy is desired, repeat with remaining flour paste. Serve over pasta.

MINESTRONE ALLA MILANESE

Makes 8 servings

2 cans (about 14 ounces *each*) beef broth

1 can (about 14 ounces) diced tomatoes

1 cup diced red potatoes

1 cup coarsely chopped carrots

1 cup coarsely chopped green cabbage

1 cup sliced zucchini

½ cup chopped onion

½ cup sliced fresh green beans

½ cup coarsely chopped celery

½ cup water

2 tablespoons olive oil

1 clove garlic, minced

½ teaspoon dried basil

¼ teaspoon dried rosemary

1 whole bay leaf

1 can (about 15 ounces) cannellini beans, rinsed and drained

Grated Parmesan cheese (optional)

1. Combine broth, tomatoes, potatoes, carrots, cabbage, zucchini, onion, green beans, celery, water, oil, garlic, basil, rosemary and bay leaf in **CROCK-POT®** slow cooker; stir to blend. Cover; cook on LOW 5 to 6 hours.

2. Add cannellini beans. Cover; cook on LOW 1 hour or until vegetables are tender.

3. Remove and discard bay leaf. Top with cheese, if desired.

ITALIAN BEEF AND BARLEY SOUP

Makes 6 servings

1 tablespoon vegetable oil

1 boneless beef top sirloin steak (about 1½ pounds), cut into 1-inch pieces

4 medium carrots or parsnips, cut into ¼-inch slices

1 cup chopped onion

1 teaspoon dried thyme

½ teaspoon dried rosemary

¼ teaspoon black pepper

⅓ cup uncooked pearl barley

2 cans (about 14 ounces *each*) beef broth

1 can (about 14 ounces) diced tomatoes with Italian seasoning, undrained

1. Heat oil over medium-high heat in large skillet. Add beef; cook 6 to 8 minutes or until browned on all sides.

2. Place carrots and onion in **CROCK-POT®** slow cooker; sprinkle with thyme, rosemary and pepper. Top with barley and beef. Pour broth and tomatoes over beef.

3. Cover; cook on LOW 8 to 10 hours or until beef is tender.

TIP: Choose pearl barley rather than quick-cooking barley, because it will stand up to the long cooking time.

HEARTY WHITE BEAN MINESTRONE

Makes 6 servings

5 cups vegetable broth

2 cans (about 15 ounces *each*) cannellini beans, rinsed and drained

1 can (about 14 ounces) diced tomatoes

2 medium russet potatoes (about 6 ounces *each*), peeled and cut into ½-inch cubes

3 medium stalks celery, chopped

3 medium carrots, chopped

1 medium onion, chopped

3 cloves garlic, minced

6 cups chopped fresh kale

6 tablespoons grated Parmesan cheese

1. Combine broth, beans, tomatoes, potatoes, celery, carrots, onion and garlic in **CROCK-POT®** slow cooker; stir to blend. Cover; cook on LOW 7 hours.

2. Turn **CROCK-POT®** slow cooker to HIGH. Stir in kale. Cover; cook on HIGH 1 to 2 hours. Top each serving with cheese.

ITALIAN WEDDING SOUP WITH THREE-CHEESE TORTELLINI

Makes 8 servings

6 cups chicken broth

1 package (16 ounces) frozen Italian-style meatballs

2½ cups kale, stemmed and chopped

1 package (9 ounces) refrigerated three-cheese tortellini

1 cup celery, chopped

1 small onion, thinly sliced

1 teaspoon dried basil

Juice of 1 lemon

1 tablespoon minced garlic

⅛ teaspoon salt

⅛ teaspoon sugar

Salt and black pepper

Combine broth, meatballs, kale, tortellini, celery, onion, basil, lemon juice, garlic, salt, sugar and pepper in **CROCK-POT®** slow cooker; stir to blend. Cover; cook on LOW 3 to 4 hours, stirring halfway through cooking time.

PESTO, WHITE BEAN AND PASTA STEW

Makes 6 servings

1 can (28 ounces) Italian seasoned diced tomatoes

2 cups vegetable broth

1 green bell pepper, chopped

1 cup uncooked elbow macaroni or ditalini pasta

1 can (about 15 ounces) cannellini or Great Northern beans, rinsed and drained

¼ cup prepared basil pesto

⅓ cup grated Parmesan or Romano cheese

1. Coat inside of **CROCK-POT®** slow cooker with nonstick cooking spray. Combine tomatoes, broth, bell pepper and pasta in **CROCK-POT®** slow cooker; stir to blend. Cover; cook on LOW 4 to 5 hours or on HIGH 2 to 2½ hours.

2. Stir in beans and pesto. Cover; cook on HIGH 10 to 15 minutes or until heated through. Ladle into shallow bowls; top with cheese.

ZUPPA DE CLAMS

Makes 3 to 4 servings

1 package (8 ounces) shiitake mushrooms

1 red onion, diced

½ pound chorizo sausage, thinly sliced

1½ cups tomato sauce

1 cup dry white wine

½ cup sweet red vermouth

24 littleneck clams, scrubbed and rinsed

Hot cooked pasta (optional)

Crusty Italian bread (optional)

1. Heat large skillet over medium heat. Add mushrooms, onion and sausage; cook and stir 8 minutes or until onion is softened. Remove to **CROCK-POT®** slow cooker.

2. Add tomato sauce, wine and vermouth to **CROCK-POT®** slow cooker. Cover; cook on LOW 6 to 7 hours or on HIGH 3 to 4 hours. Add clams; cover and cook on HIGH 10 to 15 minutes or until clams open. Discard any clams that do not open. Serve over pasta and with bread, if desired.

ITALIAN-STYLE TURKEY SAUSAGE

Makes 5 servings

1 package (about 1 pound) Italian turkey sausage, cut into 1-inch pieces

1 can (about 15 ounces) pinto beans, rinsed and drained

1 cup meatless pasta sauce

1 medium green bell pepper, cut into strips

1 small yellow onion, halved and sliced

½ teaspoon salt

¼ teaspoon black pepper

Fresh basil leaves (optional)

Italian bread (optional)

1. Brown sausage in large skillet over medium-high heat 6 to 8 minutes. Drain fat.

2. Place sausage, beans, pasta sauce, bell pepper, onion, salt and black pepper in **CROCK-POT®** slow cooker. Cover; cook on LOW 4 to 6 hours or on HIGH 2 to 3 hours. Garnish with basil. Serve with bread, if desired.

PASTA FAGIOLI SOUP

Makes 5 to 6 servings

2 cans (about 14 ounces *each*) vegetable broth

1 can (about 15 ounces) Great Northern beans, rinsed and drained

1 can (about 14 ounces) diced tomatoes

2 zucchini, quartered lengthwise and sliced

1 tablespoon olive oil

1½ teaspoons minced garlic

½ teaspoon dried basil

½ teaspoon dried oregano

½ cup uncooked ditalini, tubetti or small shell pasta

½ cup garlic-seasoned croutons

½ cup grated Asiago or Romano cheese

3 tablespoons chopped fresh basil or Italian parsley (optional)

1. Combine broth, beans, tomatoes, zucchini, oil, garlic, dried basil and oregano in **CROCK-POT®** slow cooker; stir to blend. Cover; cook on LOW 3 to 4 hours.

2. Stir in pasta. Cover; cook on LOW 1 hour or until pasta is tender. Serve soup with croutons and cheese. Garnish with fresh basil.

TIP: Only small pasta varieties should be used in this recipe. The low heat of a **CROCK-POT®** slow cooker will not allow larger pasta shapes to cook completely.

ITALIAN SAUSAGE SOUP

Makes 4 to 6 servings

1 pound mild Italian sausage, casings removed

½ cup dry bread crumbs

¼ cup grated Parmesan cheese, plus additional for garnish

¼ cup milk

1 egg

½ teaspoon dried basil

½ teaspoon black pepper

¼ teaspoon garlic salt

4 cups hot chicken broth

1 tablespoon tomato paste

1 clove garlic, minced

¼ teaspoon red pepper flakes

½ cup uncooked mini pasta shells*

1 bag (10 ounces) baby spinach leaves

*Or use other tiny pasta, such as ditalini (mini tubes) or farfallini (mini bowties).

1. Combine sausage, bread crumbs, ¼ cup cheese, milk, egg, basil, black pepper and garlic salt in large bowl; mix well. Shape sausage mixture into ½-inch balls.

2. Combine broth, tomato paste, garlic and red pepper flakes in **CROCK-POT®** slow cooker. Add meatballs. Cover; cook on LOW 5 to 6 hours.

3. Add pasta; cook on LOW 30 minutes. Stir in spinach leaves when pasta is tender. Ladle into bowls; sprinkle with additional cheese.

CANNELLINI MINESTRONE SOUP

Makes 6 servings

4 cups chicken broth

2 cups escarole, cut into ribbons

1 can (about 14 ounces) diced tomatoes

1 can (12 ounces) tomato-vegetable juice

1 cup chopped green onions

1 cup chopped carrots

1 cup chopped celery

1 cup chopped potatoes

¼ cup dried cannellini beans, rinsed and sorted

2 tablespoons chopped fresh chives

1 tablespoon chopped fresh Italian parsley

¼ teaspoon salt

¼ teaspoon black pepper

2 ounces uncooked ditalini pasta

1. Combine broth, escarole, tomatoes, vegetable juice, green onions, carrots, celery, potatoes, beans, chives, parsley, salt and pepper in **CROCK-POT®** slow cooker; stir to blend. Cover; cook on LOW 6 to 8 hours or on HIGH 4 to 6 hours.

2. Stir in pasta. Cover; cook on HIGH 20 minutes or until pasta is tender.

ITALIAN FISH SOUP

Makes 4 servings

1 can (about 14 ounces) Italian-seasoned diced tomatoes	½ teaspoon crushed saffron threads (optional)
1 can (about 14 ounces) chicken broth	¼ teaspoon red pepper flakes
1 small fennel bulb, chopped (about 1 cup), fronds reserved for garnish	½ pound (8 ounces) skinless halibut or cod fillets, cut into 1-inch pieces
3 cloves garlic, minced	½ pound (8 ounces) raw medium shrimp, peeled and deveined (with tails on)
1 tablespoon olive oil	
½ teaspoon dried basil	

1. Combine tomatoes, broth, fennel bulb, garlic, oil, basil, saffron, if desired, and red pepper flakes in **CROCK-POT®** slow cooker; stir to blend. Cover; cook on LOW 4 to 5 hours or on HIGH 2½ to 3 hours.

2. Stir in halibut and shrimp. Cover; cook on HIGH 15 to 30 minutes or until shrimp are pink and opaque and fish begins to flake when tested with fork. Ladle soup evenly into shallow bowls. Garnish with fennel fronds.

CHICKEN & TURKEY

CHICKEN SCALOPPINE IN ALFREDO SAUCE

Makes 6 servings

2 tablespoons all-purpose flour

¼ teaspoon salt

¼ teaspoon black pepper

6 boneless, skinless chicken tenderloins (about 1 pound), cut lengthwise in half

1 tablespoon butter

1 tablespoon olive oil

1 cup Alfredo pasta sauce

1 package (12 ounces) uncooked spinach noodles

1. Place flour, salt and pepper in large bowl; stir to combine. Add chicken; toss to coat. Heat butter and oil in large skillet over medium-high heat. Add chicken; cook 3 minutes per side or until browned. Remove chicken in single layer to **CROCK-POT®** slow cooker.

2. Add Alfredo pasta sauce to **CROCK-POT®** slow cooker. Cover; cook on LOW 1 to 1½ hours.

3. Meanwhile, cook noodles according to package directions. Drain; place in large shallow bowl. Spoon chicken and sauce over noodles.

BRAISED ITALIAN CHICKEN WITH TOMATOES AND OLIVES

Makes 4 servings

2 pounds boneless, skinless chicken thighs

1 teaspoon kosher salt

½ teaspoon black pepper

½ cup all-purpose flour

Olive oil

1 can (about 14 ounces) diced tomatoes, drained

⅓ cup pitted kalamata olives, quartered

⅓ cup dry red wine

1 clove garlic, minced

1 teaspoon chopped fresh rosemary

½ teaspoon red pepper flakes

Hot cooked linguini or spaghetti

Grated Parmesan cheese (optional)

1. Season chicken with salt and black pepper. Spread flour on plate; lightly dredge chicken in flour, coating both sides.

2. Heat oil in large skillet over medium heat. Working in batches, brown chicken on both sides. Use additional oil as needed to prevent sticking. Remove to **CROCK-POT®** slow cooker.

3. Add tomatoes, olives, wine and garlic. Cover; cook on LOW 4 to 5 hours.

4. Stir rosemary and red pepper flakes into **CROCK-POT®** slow cooker. Cover; cook on LOW 1 hour. Serve over linguini. Garnish with cheese.

TURKEY PICCATA

Makes 4 servings

2½ tablespoons all-purpose flour

¼ teaspoon salt

¼ teaspoon black pepper

1 pound turkey breast meat, cut into strips*

1 tablespoon butter

1 tablespoon olive oil

½ cup chicken broth

2 teaspoons lemon juice

   Grated peel of 1 lemon

2 cups hot cooked rice (optional)

2 tablespoons finely chopped fresh Italian parsley

*You may substitute turkey tenderloins.

1. Combine flour, salt and pepper in large resealable food storage bag. Add turkey. Seal bag; shake to coat. Heat butter and oil in large skillet over medium-high heat. Add turkey in single layer; brown on all sides. Remove to **CROCK-POT®** slow cooker.

2. Pour broth into skillet, stirring to scrape up any browned bits. Pour into **CROCK-POT®** slow cooker. Add lemon juice and peel to **CROCK-POT®** slow cooker. Cover; cook on LOW 1 hour. Serve over rice, if desired. Garnish with parsley.

TIP: This recipe will also work with chicken strips. Start with boneless, skinless chicken breasts, then follow the recipe as directed.

MINI PUTTANESCA MEATBALLS AND SPAGHETTI

Makes 8 servings

1 **pound ground turkey**

¼ **cup seasoned dry bread crumbs**

1 **egg**

1 **jar (24 to 26 ounces) marinara sauce**

½ **cup coarsely chopped pitted kalamata olives**

2 **tablespoons drained capers**

½ **to ¾ teaspoon red pepper flakes**

6 **ounces hot cooked spaghetti**

¼ **cup fresh basil or Italian parsley slivers (optional)**

1. Preheat oven to 425°F. Combine turkey, bread crumbs and egg in large bowl; mix well. Shape into 24 (1-inch) meatballs; place on foil-lined baking sheet. Bake 15 to 18 minutes or until browned and no longer pink in center.

2. Coat inside of 2-quart **CROCK-POT®** slow cooker with nonstick cooking spray. Combine marinara sauce, olives, capers and red pepper flakes in **CROCK-POT®** slow cooker; stir to blend. Add meatballs. Cover; cook on LOW 3 to 4 hours or on HIGH 1½ to 2 hours. Serve sauce and meatballs with spaghetti. Top with basil.

CHICKEN MARSALA WITH FETTUCCINE

Makes 6 to 8 servings

4 boneless, skinless chicken breasts

1 tablespoon vegetable oil

1 onion, chopped

½ cup Marsala wine

2 packages (6 ounces *each*) sliced cremini mushrooms

½ cup chicken broth

2 teaspoons Worcestershire sauce

½ teaspoon salt

½ teaspoon black pepper

½ cup whipping cream

2 tablespoons cornstarch

8 ounces fettuccine, cooked and drained

2 tablespoons chopped fresh Italian parsley (optional)

1. Coat inside of **CROCK-POT®** slow cooker with nonstick cooking spray. Arrange chicken in single layer in **CROCK-POT®** slow cooker.

2. Heat oil in large skillet over medium heat. Add onion; cook and stir until translucent. Add wine; cook 2 minutes or until mixture reduces slightly. Stir in mushrooms, broth, Worcestershire sauce, salt and pepper. Pour mixture over chicken. Cover; cook on HIGH 1½ to 1¾ hours or until chicken is cooked through.

3. Remove chicken to large cutting board. Cover loosely with foil to keep warm. Stir cream into cornstarch in small bowl until smooth. Whisk into cooking liquid. Cover; cook on HIGH 15 minutes or until thickened. Slice chicken. Place fettuccine in large serving bowl. Top with chicken and sauce. Garnish with parsley.

TIP: Skinless chicken is usually best for recipes using the **CROCK-POT®** slow cooker, because the skin can shrivel and curl during cooking.

CHICKEN VESUVIO

Makes 4 to 6 servings

3 tablespoons all-purpose flour

1½ teaspoons dried oregano

1 teaspoon salt

½ teaspoon black pepper

1 frying chicken, cut up and trimmed *or* 3 pounds bone-in chicken pieces, trimmed

2 tablespoons olive oil

4 small baking potatoes, unpeeled and cut into 8 wedges *each*

2 small onions, cut into thin wedges

4 cloves garlic, minced

¼ cup chicken broth

¼ cup dry white wine

¼ cup chopped fresh Italian parsley Lemon wedges (optional)

1. Combine flour, oregano, salt and pepper in large resealable food storage bag. Add chicken, several pieces at a time, to bag; shake to coat lightly with flour mixture. Heat oil in large skillet over medium heat. Add chicken; cook 10 to 12 minutes or until browned on all sides.

2. Place potatoes, onions and garlic in **CROCK-POT**® slow cooker. Add broth and wine; top with chicken pieces. Pour pan juices from skillet over chicken. Cover; cook on LOW 6 to 7 hours or on HIGH 3 to 3½ hours.

3. Remove chicken and vegetables to serving plates; top with juices from **CROCK-POT**® slow cooker. Sprinkle with parsley. Serve with lemon wedges, if desired.

BRAISED TURKEY BREASTS WITH LEMON-ARTICHOKE HEART SAUCE

Makes 6 servings

- 2 **bone-in, skin-on turkey breasts (about 2 pounds** *each***)**
- 2 **teaspoons salt, plus additional for seasoning**
- ¼ **teaspoon black pepper, plus additional for seasoning**
- ½ **cup all-purpose flour**
- 4 **teaspoons vegetable oil, divided**
- 4 **large shallots, peeled and thinly sliced**
- ½ **cup dry sherry**

- 1 **lemon, sliced into ¼-inch-thick slices**
- 2 **tablespoons capers, rinsed and drained**
- 4 **sprigs fresh thyme**
- 1½ **cups chicken broth**
- 2 **cans (about 14 ounces** *each***) artichoke hearts, drained**
- 2 **tablespoons finely chopped fresh Italian parsley**

  Hot cooked egg noodles

1. Season both sides of turkey breasts with salt and pepper. Dredge in flour, shaking off excess. Heat 2 teaspoons oil in large skillet over medium-high heat. Add 1 turkey breast; cook 4 minutes or until brown on both sides. Remove to **CROCK-POT®** slow cooker. Repeat with remaining 2 teaspoons oil and second turkey breast; remove to **CROCK-POT®** slow cooker.

2. Reduce heat to medium. Add shallots to skillet; cook 4 minutes or until softened and just beginning to brown. Add sherry; cook 30 seconds or until pan is almost dry, stirring to scrape up any browned bits from bottom of pan. Pour shallot mixture over turkey breasts. Add lemon slices, capers, thyme sprigs, 2 teaspoons salt and ¼ teaspoon pepper. Pour in broth. Cover; cook on LOW 6 hours or until turkey breasts are tender and nearly falling off the bone.

3. Remove turkey breasts to large cutting board. Cover loosely with foil; let stand 10 to 15 minutes. Remove and discard skin and bones.

4. Remove thyme from cooking liquid; discard. Let cooking liquid stand 5 minutes. Skim off and discard fat. Stir in artichoke hearts and parsley. Season to taste with salt and pepper. Slice turkey. Serve over noodles topped with sauce.

BONELESS CHICKEN CACCIATORE

Makes 6 servings

Olive oil

6 boneless, skinless chicken breasts, sliced in half horizontally

4 cups tomato-basil pasta sauce

1 cup coarsely chopped yellow onion

1 cup coarsely chopped green bell pepper

1 can (6 ounces) sliced mushrooms

¼ cup dry red wine

2 teaspoons minced garlic

2 teaspoons dried oregano

2 teaspoons dried thyme

2 teaspoons salt

2 teaspoons black pepper

Hot cooked pasta

1. Heat oil in large skillet over medium heat. Add chicken; cook 6 to 8 minutes or until browned on both sides. Remove to **CROCK-POT®** slow cooker using slotted spoon.

2. Add pasta sauce, onion, bell pepper, mushrooms, wine, garlic, oregano, thyme, salt and black pepper to **CROCK-POT®** slow cooker; stir to blend. Cover; cook on LOW 5 to 7 hours or on HIGH 2 to 3 hours. Serve over pasta.

CREAM CHEESE CHICKEN WITH BROCCOLI

Makes 10 to 12 servings

4 pounds boneless, skinless chicken breasts, cut into ½-inch pieces

1 tablespoon olive oil

1 package (1 ounce) Italian salad dressing mix

Nonstick cooking spray

2 cups (about 8 ounces) sliced mushrooms

1 cup chopped onion

1 can (10½ ounces) condensed cream of chicken soup, undiluted

1 bag (10 ounces) frozen broccoli florets, thawed

1 package (8 ounces) cream cheese, cubed

¼ cup dry sherry

Hot cooked pasta

1. Toss chicken with oil in large bowl. Sprinkle with salad dressing mix. Remove to **CROCK-POT®** slow cooker. Cover; cook on LOW 3 hours.

2. Spray large skillet with cooking spray; heat over medium heat. Add mushrooms and onion; cook and stir 5 minutes or until onion is tender.

3. Add soup, broccoli, cream cheese and sherry to skillet; cook and stir until heated through. Remove to **CROCK-POT®** slow cooker. Cover; cook on LOW 1 hour. Serve chicken and sauce over pasta.

TIP: For easier preparation, cut up the chicken and vegetables for this recipe the night before. Wrap the chicken and vegetables separately, and store in the refrigerator.

CHICKEN PARMESAN WITH EGGPLANT

Makes 6 to 8 servings

6 boneless, skinless chicken breasts

2 eggs

2 teaspoons salt

2 teaspoons black pepper

2 cups seasoned dry bread crumbs

½ cup olive oil

½ cup (1 stick) butter

2 small eggplants, cut into ¾-inch-thick slices

1½ cups grated Parmesan cheese

2¼ cups tomato-basil pasta sauce

1 pound sliced or shredded mozzarella cheese

Sprigs fresh basil (optional)

1. Slice chicken breasts in half lengthwise. Cut each half lengthwise again to get four ¾-inch slices.

2. Combine eggs, salt and pepper in medium bowl; whisk to blend. Place bread crumbs in separate medium bowl. Dip chicken in egg mixture; turn to coat. Then coat chicken with bread crumbs, covering both sides evenly.

3. Heat oil and butter in large skillet over medium heat. Add breaded chicken; cook 6 to 8 minutes until browned on both sides. Remove to paper towel-lined plate to drain excess oil.

4. Layer half of eggplant, ¾ cup Parmesan cheese and 1 cup sauce in bottom of **CROCK-POT®** slow cooker. Top with half of chicken, remaining half of eggplant, remaining ¾ cup Parmesan cheese and ¼ cup sauce. Arrange remaining half of chicken on sauce; top with remaining 1 cup sauce and mozzarella cheese. Cover; cook on LOW 6 hours or on HIGH 2 to 4 hours. Garnish with fresh basil.

TURKEY BREAST AND MUSHROOM RISOTTO

Makes 8 servings

3¾ cups chicken broth

4 tablespoons (½ stick) butter, divided

1 onion, chopped

2 cloves garlic, minced

1¼ cups uncooked Arborio rice

½ cup dry white wine

2 packages (10 ounces *each*) mushrooms, sliced and divided

8 turkey breast cutlets (6 ounces *each* and ½ inch thick)

1 teaspoon salt

½ teaspoon black pepper

Smoked paprika

Grated Parmesan cheese and ground sage (optional)

1. Coat inside of **CROCK-POT®** slow cooker with nonstick cooking spray. Bring broth to a boil in medium saucepan over medium-high heat.

2. Melt 2 tablespoons butter in small skillet over medium-high heat. Add onion; cook and stir 3 to 4 minutes or until translucent. Add garlic; cook 30 seconds. Stir in rice; cook and stir 3 minutes. Add wine; cook and stir 2 to 3 minutes or until absorbed. Remove mixture to **CROCK-POT®** slow cooker. Stir in broth and 6 cups mushrooms.

3. Season turkey with salt and pepper; place in **CROCK-POT®** slow cooker. Cover; cook on LOW 3½ to 4 hours or on HIGH 1¾ hours to 2 hours or until turkey is cooked through and rice is tender.* Sprinkle turkey with smoked paprika.

4. Melt remaining 2 tablespoons butter in small skillet over medium-high heat. Add remaining mushrooms; cook and stir 5 minutes or until golden brown. Serve turkey and risotto with mushrooms. Top with cheese and sage, if desired.

*If rice is not tender, remove the turkey and keep warm. Continue cooking rice, checking every 15 minutes.

CHICKEN SALTIMBOCCA-STYLE

Makes 6 servings

6 boneless, skinless chicken breasts

12 slices prosciutto

12 slices provolone cheese

½ cup all-purpose flour

½ cup grated Parmesan cheese

2 teaspoons salt

2 teaspoons black pepper

Olive oil

2 cans (10¾ ounces *each*) condensed cream of mushroom soup, undiluted

¾ cup dry white wine

1 teaspoon ground sage

1. Split each chicken breast into two thin pieces. Place between two pieces of waxed paper or plastic wrap; pound until ⅓ inch thick. Place 1 slice of prosciutto and 1 slice of provolone on each chicken piece and roll up. Secure with toothpicks.

2. Combine flour, Parmesan cheese, salt and pepper on large rimmed plate. Dredge chicken in flour mixture, shaking off excess. Reserve excess flour mixture. Heat oil in large skillet over medium heat. Add chicken; cook 5 to 7 minutes or until browned on both sides. Remove to **CROCK-POT®** slow cooker. Add soup, wine and sage.

3. Cover; cook on LOW 5 to 7 hours or on HIGH 2 to 3 hours. Remove chicken to large serving platter. Whisk 2 to 3 tablespoons reserved flour mixture into cooking liquid. Cover; cook on HIGH 15 minutes or until thickened. Serve chicken with sauce.

BASIL CHICKEN MERLOT WITH WILD MUSHROOMS

Makes 4 to 6 servings

3 tablespoons extra virgin olive oil, divided

1 roasting chicken (about 3 pounds), skinned and cut up

1½ cups thickly sliced cremini mushrooms

1 medium yellow onion, diced

2 cloves garlic, minced

1 cup chicken broth

1 can (6 ounces) tomato paste

⅓ cup Merlot or dry red wine

2 teaspoons sugar

1 teaspoon ground oregano

¼ teaspoon salt

¼ teaspoon black pepper

2 tablespoons minced fresh basil

3 cups hot cooked ziti pasta, drained

1. Heat 1½ to 2 tablespoons oil in skillet over medium heat. Working in batches, brown chicken pieces on each side 3 to 5 minutes, turning once. Remove to plate using slotted spoon.

2. Heat remaining oil in skillet. Add mushrooms, onion and garlic; cook and stir 7 to 8 minutes or until onion is soft. Remove to **CROCK-POT®** slow cooker. Top with chicken.

3. Combine broth, tomato paste, wine, sugar, oregano, salt and pepper in medium bowl. Pour sauce over chicken. Cover; cook on LOW 7 to 9 hours or on HIGH 3 to 4 hours.

4. Stir in basil. Place pasta in serving bowls. Ladle chicken, mushrooms and sauce evenly over pasta.

CHICKEN MARBELLA

Makes 10 servings

- 10 boneless, skinless chicken breasts (6 ounces *each*)
- 1 teaspoon salt
- ¼ teaspoon black pepper
- 2 tablespoons olive oil
- ¾ cup dry white wine
- ½ cup balsamic vinegar
- 12 cloves garlic, crushed
- 1 cup dried figs or prunes, halved lengthwise
- ¾ cup packed brown sugar
- ½ cup black olives
- 1 jar (3½ ounces) capers, drained and juice reserved
- 6 whole bay leaves
- 1 teaspoon dried oregano
- 1 tablespoon plus 1½ teaspoons cornstarch

1. Season chicken with salt and pepper. Heat oil in large skillet over medium-high heat. Cook chicken in batches 4 to 5 minutes or until browned on both sides. Place chicken in **CROCK-POT®** slow cooker. Add wine and vinegar to skillet, scraping up any browned bits. Pour over chicken.

2. Add garlic, figs, brown sugar, olives, capers, 2 teaspoons reserved caper juice and bay leaves to **CROCK-POT®** slow cooker. Cover; cook on LOW 3 to 4 hours or on HIGH 1½ to 2 hours.

3. Remove chicken to large serving plate; keep warm. Strain cooking liquid through sieve into large bowl. Remove and discard bay leaves; reserve figs, olives and capers. Stir oregano into liquid. Return liquid to **CROCK-POT®** slow cooker. Whisk ¼ cup liquid into cornstarch in small bowl until smooth. Whisk into cooking liquid in **CROCK-POT®** slow cooker. Cook, uncovered, on HIGH 10 to 15 minutes or until thickened. Serve chicken with reserved figs, olives and capers. Top with sauce.

CREAMY PESTO AND SUN-DRIED TOMATO CHICKEN

Makes 6 servings

2 teaspoons butter

1 teaspoon olive oil

6 boneless, skinless chicken breasts (about 1½ pounds)

½ cup sun-dried tomatoes, packed in oil and chopped

½ cup pesto, oil drained

½ cup chicken broth

1 package (1 ounce) ranch seasoning mix

¼ cup half-and-half

1. Coat inside of **CROCK-POT®** slow cooker with nonstick cooking spray. Heat butter and oil in large skillet over medium-high heat. Add chicken; brown 3 to 4 minutes on each side.

2. Place chicken, tomatoes, pesto, broth and seasoning mix in **CROCK-POT®** slow cooker. Cover; cook on LOW 6 hours or on HIGH 3 to 4 hours. Stir in half-and-half.

SERVING SUGGESTION: Serve with a mixed green salad, pasta, potatoes or couscous.

CHICKEN WITH MUSHROOMS

Makes 4 servings

8 boneless, skinless chicken breasts (2 pounds *total*), cut into pieces

3 cups sliced mushrooms

1 large onion, chopped

1 can (6 ounces) tomato paste

½ cup chicken broth

¼ cup dry red wine

2 tablespoons quick-cooking tapioca

2 cloves garlic, minced

2 teaspoons sugar

2 teaspoons dried basil

Salt and black pepper

Hot cooked noodles (optional)

Grated Parmesan cheese (optional)

Place chicken, mushrooms, onion, tomato paste, broth, wine, tapioca, garlic, sugar, basil, salt and pepper in **CROCK-POT®** slow cooker. Cover; cook on LOW 7 to 8 hours or on HIGH 3 to 4 hours. Serve over noodles, if desired. Garnish with cheese.

TURKEY SPINACH LASAGNA

Makes 8 servings

Nonstick cooking spray

¾ cup chopped onion

2 cloves garlic, minced

1 pound ground turkey

1 teaspoon Italian seasoning

¼ teaspoon black pepper

1 container (15 ounces) ricotta cheese

1 cup (4 ounces) Italian shredded cheese blend, divided

12 ounces no-boil lasagna noodles

1 package (10 ounces) frozen chopped spinach, thawed and pressed dry

1 jar (24 to 26 ounces) chunky marinara sauce

½ cup water

1. Spray large skillet with cooking spray; heat over medium heat. Add onion and garlic; cook and stir 4 minutes. Add turkey; cook and stir until no longer pink, stirring to break up meat. Season with Italian seasoning and pepper; remove from heat. Set aside.

2. Combine ricotta cheese and ½ cup Italian cheese in small bowl; mix well.

3. Layer half of uncooked noodles, breaking in half to fit and overlap as necessary, in **CROCK-POT**® slow cooker. Spread half of meat mixture and half of spinach over noodles. Top with half of marinara sauce and ¼ cup water. Gently spread cheese mixture on top. Repeat layers with remaining noodles, meat mixture, spinach, marinara sauce and ¼ cup water.

4. Cover; cook on LOW 4 hours. To serve, sprinkle top with remaining ½ cup Italian cheese. Cover; cook on LOW 10 to 15 minutes or until cheese is melted. Divide evenly into eight pieces.

BEEF & PORK

ITALIAN BRAISED SHORT RIBS IN RED WINE

Makes 4 to 6 servings

3 pounds beef short ribs, trimmed
  Salt and black pepper
1 tablespoon vegetable oil, plus additional as needed
2 onions, sliced
2 packages (8 ounces *each*) cremini mushrooms, quartered

2 cups dry red wine
2 cups beef broth
2 teaspoons Italian seasoning
2 cloves garlic, minced
  Mashed potatoes or polenta

1. Coat inside of **CROCK-POT®** slow cooker with nonstick cooking spray. Season short ribs with salt and pepper. Heat 1 tablespoon oil in large skillet over medium-high heat. Working in batches, brown ribs on all sides, adding additional oil as needed. Remove to **CROCK-POT®** slow cooker.

2. Return skillet to heat. Add onions; cook and stir 3 minutes or until translucent. Stir in mushrooms, wine, broth, Italian seasoning and garlic; bring to a simmer. Simmer 3 minutes; pour over short ribs. Cover; cook on LOW 10 to 12 hours or on HIGH 6 to 8 hours. Season with salt and pepper. Remove ribs and mushrooms to large serving platter. Strain cooking liquid; serve ribs with mashed potatoes and cooking liquid.

PASTA SHELLS WITH PROSCIUTTO

Makes 4 servings

3 cups (8 ounces) uncooked medium shell pasta

1 jar (24 to 26 ounces) vodka pasta sauce

¾ cup water

½ cup whipping cream

2 ounces (½ cup) torn or coarsely chopped thin sliced prosciutto

¼ cup chopped fresh chives

1. Coat inside of **CROCK-POT®** slow cooker with nonstick cooking spray. Combine pasta, pasta sauce and water in **CROCK-POT®** slow cooker; stir to blend. Cover; cook on LOW 2 hours or on HIGH 1 hour.

2. Stir in cream. Cover; cook on LOW 1 to 1½ hours or on HIGH 45 minutes to 1 hour or until pasta is tender.

3. Stir prosciutto into pasta mixture. Spoon into shallow bowls; top with chives.

RIGATONI WITH BROCCOLI RABE AND SAUSAGE

Makes 6 servings

2 tablespoons olive oil

3 sweet or hot Italian sausage links, casings removed

2 cloves garlic, minced

1 large bunch (about 1¼ pounds) broccoli rabe

½ cup chicken broth

1 teaspoon salt

½ teaspoon red pepper flakes

1 pound uncooked rigatoni

Grated Parmesan cheese (optional)

1. Coat inside of **CROCK-POT®** slow cooker with nonstick cooking spray.

2. Heat oil in large skillet over medium heat. Add sausage; cook and stir 6 to 8 minutes, stirring to break up meat. Drain fat. Add garlic; cook and stir 1 minute or until softened and fragrant. Remove to **CROCK-POT®** slow cooker.

3. Trim any stiff, woody parts from bottoms of broccoli rabe stems; discard. Cut broccoli rabe into 1-inch lengths. Place in large bowl of cold water; stir with hands to wash well. Lift broccoli rabe out of water by handfuls leaving any sand or dirt in bottom of bowl. Shake well to remove excess water, but do not dry. Add to **CROCK-POT®** slow cooker with sausage. Add broth, salt and red pepper flakes. Cover; cook on LOW 4 hours or on HIGH 2 hours.

4. Meanwhile, cook rigatoni according to package directions. Stir into sausage mixture just before serving. Garnish with cheese.

ITALIAN MEATBALL HOAGIES

Makes 4 servings

½ pound ground beef

½ pound Italian sausage, casings removed

¼ cup seasoned dry bread crumbs

¼ cup grated Parmesan cheese

1 egg

1 tablespoon olive oil

1 cup pasta sauce

2 tablespoons tomato paste

¼ teaspoon red pepper flakes (optional)

4 (6-inch) hoagie rolls, split and lightly toasted

1 cup (4 ounces) shredded mozzarella cheese

1. Coat inside of **CROCK-POT®** slow cooker with nonstick cooking spray. Combine beef, sausage, bread crumbs, Parmesan cheese and egg in large bowl; mix well. Shape to form 16 (1½-inch) meatballs.

2. Heat oil in large skillet over medium heat. Add meatballs; cook 6 to 8 minutes or until browned on all sides, turning occasionally. Remove meatballs to **CROCK-POT®** slow cooker using slotted spoon.

3. Combine pasta sauce, tomato paste and red pepper flakes, if desired, in medium bowl; stir to blend. Spoon over meatballs; gently toss.

4. Cover; cook on LOW 5 to 7 hours or on HIGH 2½ to 3 hours. Place meatballs in rolls. Spoon sauce over meatballs; top with mozzarella cheese.

SLOW COOKER PIZZA CASSEROLE

Makes 6 servings

1½ pounds ground beef

1 pound bulk pork sausage

4 jars (14 ounces *each*) pizza sauce

2 cups (8 ounces) shredded mozzarella cheese

2 cups grated Parmesan cheese

2 cans (4 ounces *each*) mushroom stems and pieces, drained

2 packages (3 ounces *each*) sliced pepperoni

½ cup finely chopped onion

½ cup finely chopped green bell pepper

1 clove garlic, minced

1 pound corkscrew pasta, cooked and drained

1. Brown beef and sausage in large nonstick skillet over medium-high heat 6 to 8 minutes, stirring to break up meat. Remove beef mixture to **CROCK-POT®** slow cooker using slotted spoon.

2. Add pizza sauce, cheeses, mushrooms, pepperoni, onion, bell pepper and garlic; stir to blend. Cover; cook on LOW 3½ hours or on HIGH 2 hours.

3. Stir in pasta. Cover; cook on HIGH 15 to 20 minutes or until pasta is heated through.

ITALIAN BRACIOLE

Makes 6 servings

2 pounds beef round steak, thinly sliced

2 slices whole grain bread, toasted and crumbled

½ cup chopped onion

¼ cup grated Parmesan cheese

2 cloves garlic

3 tablespoons olive oil, divided

1 teaspoon Italian seasoning

1 egg

½ teaspoon salt

½ teaspoon black pepper

1 jar (24 to 26 ounces) tomato-basil pasta sauce

Hot cooked pasta (optional)

Chopped fresh Italian parsley (optional)

1. Coat inside of **CROCK-POT®** slow cooker with nonstick cooking spray. Place round steak on large cutting board. Pound into ¼-inch thickness; cut evenly into two pieces.

2. Combine bread, onion, cheese, garlic, 2 tablespoons oil, Italian seasoning, egg, salt and pepper in food processor or blender; pulse just until mixture is moistened but still chunky. Divide bread mixture evenly over steak pieces; roll tightly to enclose filling. Tie each with kitchen string to secure.

3. Heat remaining 1 tablespoon oil in large skillet over medium heat. Add steak rolls; cook and turn 6 minutes or until browned on all sides. Pour ½ cup pasta sauce into bottom of **CROCK-POT®** slow cooker; top with steak rolls. Top with remaining pasta sauce. Cover; cook on LOW 4 to 5 hours. Cut rolls evenly into 14 pieces. Serve over pasta, if desired. Garnish with parsley.

MEATBALLS AND SPAGHETTI SAUCE

Makes 6 to 8 servings

2 pounds ground beef

1 cup plain dry bread crumbs

1 onion, chopped

2 eggs, beaten

¼ cup minced fresh Italian parsley

4 teaspoons minced garlic, divided

½ teaspoon dry mustard

½ teaspoon black pepper

4 tablespoons olive oil, divided

1 can (28 ounces) whole tomatoes

½ cup chopped fresh basil

1 teaspoon sugar

Salt and black pepper

Hot cooked spaghetti

1. Combine beef, bread crumbs, onion, eggs, parsley, 2 teaspoons garlic, dry mustard and ½ teaspoon pepper in large bowl; mix well. Form into walnut-sized balls. Heat 2 tablespoons oil in large skillet over medium heat. Brown meatballs on all sides. Remove to **CROCK-POT**® slow cooker.

2. Combine tomatoes, basil, remaining 2 tablespoons oil, remaining 2 teaspoons garlic, sugar, salt and black pepper in medium bowl; stir to blend. Pour over meatballs, turn to coat. Cover; cook on LOW 3 to 5 hours or on HIGH 2 to 4 hours. Serve over spaghetti.

TIP: Recipe can be doubled for a 5-, 6- or 7-quart **CROCK-POT**® slow cooker.

ITALIAN-STYLE POT ROAST

Makes 6 to 8 servings

2 teaspoons minced garlic

1 teaspoon salt

1 teaspoon dried basil

1 teaspoon dried oregano

¼ teaspoon red pepper flakes

1 boneless beef bottom round rump roast or chuck shoulder roast (about 2½ to 3 pounds)*

1 large onion, quartered and thinly sliced

1½ cups tomato-basil or marinara pasta sauce

2 cans (about 15 ounces *each*) cannellini or Great Northern beans, rinsed and drained

¼ cup shredded fresh basil (optional)

Unless you have a 5-, 6- or 7-quart CROCK-POT® slow cooker, cut any roast larger than 2½ pounds in half so it cooks completely.

1. Combine garlic, salt, dried basil, oregano and red pepper flakes in small bowl; rub over roast.

2. Place onion slices in **CROCK-POT®** slow cooker. Place roast over onion slices in **CROCK-POT®** slow cooker. Pour pasta sauce over roast. Cover; cook on LOW 8 to 9 hours or until roast is fork-tender.

3. Remove roast to large cutting board. Cover loosely with foil; let stand 10 to 15 minutes. Turn off heat. Let liquid in **CROCK-POT®** slow cooker stand 5 minutes to allow fat to rise. Skim off fat.

4. Stir beans into liquid. Cover; cook on LOW 15 to 30 minutes or until beans are heated through. Slice roast across the grain into thin slices. Serve with bean mixture. Garnish with fresh basil.

BEEFY TORTELLINI

Makes 6 servings

½ pound ground beef

1 jar (24 to 26 ounces) roasted tomato and garlic pasta sauce

1 package (12 ounces) uncooked three-cheese tortellini

8 ounces sliced button or exotic mushrooms, such as oyster, shiitake and cremini

½ cup water

½ teaspoon red pepper flakes (optional)

¾ cup grated Asiago or Romano cheese

Chopped fresh Italian parsley (optional)

1. Coat inside of **CROCK-POT®** slow cooker with nonstick cooking spray. Brown beef in large skillet over medium-high heat 6 to 8 minutes, stirring to break up meat. Remove to **CROCK-POT®** slow cooker using slotted spoon.

2. Stir pasta sauce, tortellini, mushrooms, water and red pepper flakes, if desired, into **CROCK-POT®** slow cooker. Cover; cook on LOW 2 hours or on HIGH 1 hour. Stir.

3. Cover; cook on LOW 2 to 2½ hours or on HIGH ½ to 1 hour. Serve in shallow bowls topped with cheese and parsley, if desired.

ITALIAN SAUSAGE AND PEPPERS

Makes 4 servings

3 cups red, yellow and green bell pepper pieces (1 inch)

1 small onion, cut into thin wedges

3 cloves garlic, minced

4 links hot or mild Italian sausage (about 1 pound)

1 cup pasta sauce

¼ cup dry red wine

1 tablespoon water

1 tablespoon cornstarch

Hot cooked spaghetti

¼ cup shredded Parmesan or Romano cheese

1. Coat inside of **CROCK-POT®** slow cooker with nonstick cooking spray. Add bell peppers, onion and garlic. Arrange sausage over vegetables.

2. Combine pasta sauce and wine in small bowl; pour over sausage. Cover; cook on LOW 8 to 9 hours or on HIGH 4 to 5 hours or until sausage is cooked through and vegetables are very tender.

3. Remove sausage to serving platter; cover with foil to keep warm. Skim off and discard fat from cooking liquid.

4. Stir water into cornstarch in small bowl until smooth; whisk into cooking liquid. Cover; cook on HIGH 15 minutes or until sauce has thickened. Serve sauce over spaghetti and sausage; top with cheese.

TIP: To save time, look for mixed bell pepper pieces at supermarket salad bars.

ROSEMARY PORK WITH RED WINE RISOTTO

Makes 4 to 6 servings

1 boneless pork loin (about 3 pounds)*

1 teaspoon salt

1 teaspoon black pepper

2 tablespoons olive oil

6 sprigs fresh rosemary, divided

2 cups chicken broth, divided

½ cup minced onion

2 tablespoons butter, divided

3 cloves garlic, minced

1 cup uncooked Arborio rice

1 cup dry red wine

¾ cup grated Parmesan cheese

*Unless you have a 5-, 6- or 7-quart **CROCK-POT®** slow cooker, cut any roast larger than 2½ pounds in half so it cooks completely.

1. Season pork with salt and pepper. Heat oil in large skillet over medium-high heat. Add 3 sprigs rosemary; place pork roast on top. Brown pork roast 5 to 7 minutes on all sides. Remove roast and rosemary to **CROCK-POT®** slow cooker.

2. Add ¼ cup broth to skillet, stirring to scrape up browned bits. Add onion, 1 tablespoon butter and garlic; cook and stir until onion is translucent.

3. Add rice to skillet; cook and stir 2 minutes or until rice just begins to brown. Stir in wine and remaining 1¾ cups broth. Pour mixture around roast. Cover; cook on HIGH 3 to 4 hours, stirring occasionally, until roast reaches 160°F on thermometer inserted into center.

4. Remove and discard rosemary. Remove roast to large cutting board. Cover loosely with foil; let stand 10 to 15 minutes before slicing.

5. Stir remaining 1 tablespoon butter and cheese into rice. Serve risotto with roast and garnish with remaining rosemary.

BROCCOLI AND BEEF PASTA

Makes 4 servings

2 cups broccoli florets *or* 1 package (10 ounces) frozen broccoli

1 onion, thinly sliced

½ teaspoon dried basil

½ teaspoon dried oregano

½ teaspoon dried thyme

1 can (about 14 ounces) Italian-style diced tomatoes

¾ cup beef broth

1 pound ground beef

2 cloves garlic, minced

2 cups hot cooked rotini pasta

¾ cup grated Parmesan cheese, plus additional for garnish

2 tablespoons tomato paste

1. Layer broccoli, onion, basil, oregano, thyme, tomatoes and broth in **CROCK-POT®** slow cooker. Cover; cook on LOW 2½ hours.

2. Brown beef and garlic in large skillet over medium-high heat 6 to 8 minutes, stirring to break up meat. Remove to **CROCK-POT®** slow cooker using slotted spoon. Cover; cook on LOW 2 hours.

3. Stir in pasta, ¾ cup cheese and tomato paste. Cover; cook on LOW 30 minutes or until cheese is melted and mixture is heated through. Sprinkle with additional cheese.

SERVING SUGGESTION: Serve with garlic bread.

CLASSIC SPAGHETTI

Makes 6 to 8 servings

2 tablespoons olive oil

2 onions, chopped

2 green bell peppers, sliced

2 stalks celery, sliced

4 teaspoons minced garlic

3 pounds ground beef

2 carrots, diced

1 cup sliced mushrooms

1 can (28 ounces) tomato sauce

1 can (28 ounces) stewed tomatoes, undrained

3 cups water

2 tablespoons minced fresh Italian parsley

1 tablespoon sugar

1 tablespoon dried oregano

2 teaspoons salt

2 teaspoons black pepper

1 pound hot cooked spaghetti

1. Heat oil in large skillet over medium-high heat. Add onions, bell peppers, celery and garlic; cook and stir 3 to 5 minutes or until tender. Remove to **CROCK-POT®** slow cooker. Brown beef in same skillet 6 to 8 minutes, stirring to break up meat. Drain fat. Remove to **CROCK-POT®** slow cooker.

2. Add carrots, mushrooms, tomato sauce, tomatoes, water, parsley, sugar, oregano, salt and black pepper to **CROCK-POT®** slow cooker. Cover; cook on LOW 6 to 8 hours or on HIGH 3 to 5 hours. Serve sauce over spaghetti.

PIZZA-STYLE MOSTACCIOLI

Makes 4 servings

1 jar (24 to 26 ounces) marinara sauce or tomato-basil pasta sauce

½ cup water

2 cups (6 ounces) uncooked mostaccioli pasta

1 package (8 ounces) sliced mushrooms

1 small yellow or green bell pepper, finely diced

½ cup (1 ounce) sliced pepperoni, halved

1 teaspoon dried oregano

¼ teaspoon red pepper flakes

1 cup (4 ounces) shredded pizza cheese blend or Italian cheese blend

Chopped fresh oregano (optional)

Garlic bread (optional)

1. Coat inside of **CROCK-POT®** slow cooker with nonstick cooking spray. Combine marinara sauce and water in **CROCK-POT®** slow cooker. Stir in pasta, mushrooms, bell pepper, pepperoni, dried oregano and red pepper flakes; mix well. Cover; cook on LOW 2 hours or on HIGH 1 hour.

2. Stir well. Cover; cook on LOW 1½ to 2 hours or on HIGH 45 minutes to 1 hour or until pasta and vegetables are tender. Spoon into shallow bowls. Top with cheese and garnish with fresh oregano. Serve with bread, if desired.

TIP: To prevent the pasta from becoming overcooked on the bottom of the **CROCK-POT®** slow cooker, stir it halfway through cooking time.

ITALIAN-STYLE SAUSAGE WITH RICE

Makes 4 to 5 servings

1 pound mild Italian sausage links, cut into 1-inch pieces

1 can (about 15 ounces) pinto beans, rinsed and drained

1 cup pasta sauce

1 green bell pepper, cut into strips

1 small onion, halved and sliced

½ teaspoon salt

¼ teaspoon black pepper

Hot cooked rice

Fresh basil (optional)

1. Cook sausage in large nonstick skillet over medium-high heat, stirring to break up meat, until cooked through. Drain fat.

2. Combine sausage, beans, pasta sauce, bell pepper, onion, salt and black pepper in **CROCK-POT®** slow cooker. Cover; cook on LOW 4 to 6 hours or on HIGH 2 to 3 hours.

3. Serve with rice. Garnish with basil.

BOLOGNESE OVER RIGATONI

Makes 4 servings

1 **pound ground beef**

3 **cloves garlic, minced**

1 **can (about 28 ounces) diced tomatoes with basil, garlic and oregano**

½ **cup grated Pecorino Romano cheese**

½ **teaspoon black pepper**

8 **ounces rigatoni, cooked and drained**

Shaved Pecorino Romano cheese (optional)

Fresh basil (optional)

1. Brown beef in large skillet over medium-high heat 6 to 8 minutes, stirring to break up meat. Stir in garlic; cook 3 to 4 minutes. Remove beef mixture to **CROCK-POT®** slow cooker using slotted spoon. Stir in tomatoes. Cover; cook on LOW 6½ to 7 hours or on HIGH 3½ to 4 hours.

2. Stir grated cheese and pepper into sauce. Cook, uncovered, on HIGH 20 minutes or until slightly thickened. Divide rigatoni among four bowls. Top with sauce, shaved cheese and basil, if desired. Serve immediately.

VEGETARIAN DISHES

SPINACH AND RICOTTA STUFFED SHELLS

Makes 6 servings

18 uncooked jumbo pasta shells (about half of a 12-ounce package)

1 package (15 ounces) ricotta cheese

7 ounces frozen chopped spinach, thawed and squeezed dry

½ cup grated Parmesan cheese

1 egg, lightly beaten

1 clove garlic, minced

½ teaspoon salt

1 jar (24 to 26 ounces) marinara sauce

½ cup (2 ounces) shredded mozzarella cheese

1 teaspoon olive oil

1. Cook pasta shells according to package directions until almost tender. Drain well. Combine ricotta cheese, spinach, Parmesan cheese, egg, garlic and salt in medium bowl.

2. Pour ¼ cup marinara sauce in bottom of **CROCK-POT®** slow cooker. Spoon 2 to 3 tablespoons ricotta mixture into 1 pasta shell and place in bottom of **CROCK-POT®** slow cooker. Repeat with enough additional shells to cover bottom of **CROCK-POT®** slow cooker. Top with another ¼ cup marinara sauce. Repeat with remaining pasta shells, ricotta mixture and marinara sauce. Top with mozzarella cheese. Drizzle with oil. Cover; cook on HIGH 3 to 4 hours or until mozzarella cheese is melted and sauce is heated through.

MANCHEGO EGGPLANT

Makes 12 servings

1 cup all-purpose flour

4 large eggplants, peeled and sliced horizontally into ¾-inch-thick pieces

2 tablespoons olive oil

1 jar (24 to 26 ounces) roasted garlic-flavor pasta sauce

2 tablespoons Italian seasoning

1 cup (4 ounces) grated manchego cheese

1 jar (24 to 26 ounces) roasted eggplant-flavor marinara pasta sauce

Sprigs fresh basil (optional)

1. Place flour in medium shallow bowl. Add eggplants; toss to coat. Heat oil in large skillet over medium-high heat. Lightly brown eggplants in batches 3 to 4 minutes on each side.

2. Pour thin layer of garlic pasta sauce into bottom of **CROCK-POT®** slow cooker. Top with eggplant slices, Italian seasoning, cheese and marinara pasta sauce. Repeat layers until all ingredients have been used. Cover; cook on HIGH 2 hours.

HEARTY VEGETARIAN MAC AND CHEESE

Makes 6 servings

1 can (about 14 ounces) stewed tomatoes, undrained

1½ cups prepared Alfredo sauce

1½ cups shredded mozzarella cheese

8 ounces whole grain penne pasta, cooked and drained

7 ounces Italian-flavored vegetarian sausage links, ¼-inch slices

¾ cup fresh basil leaves, thinly sliced and divided

½ cup vegetable broth

½ teaspoon salt

2 tablespoons grated Parmesan cheese

Coat inside of **CROCK-POT®** slow cooker with nonstick cooking spray. Add tomatoes, Alfredo sauce, 1 cup mozzarella cheese, pasta, sausage, ½ cup basil, broth and salt to **CROCK-POT®** slow cooker; stir to blend. Top with remaining ½ cup mozzarella cheese and Parmesan cheese. Cover; cook on LOW 3½ hours or on HIGH 2 hours. Top with remaining ¼ cup basil.

SUMMER SQUASH LASAGNA

Makes 6 to 8 servings

3 tablespoons olive oil, divided

1 large onion, chopped

¼ teaspoon salt

2 cloves garlic, minced

2 medium zucchini (about 1 pound), cut lengthwise into ¼-inch strips

2 yellow squash (about 1 pound), cut lengthwise into ¼-inch strips

1 container (15 ounces) ricotta cheese

1 egg

¼ cup plus 2 tablespoons chopped fresh basil, divided

¼ teaspoon black pepper

½ cup grated Parmesan cheese, divided

1 jar (24 to 26 ounces) marinara sauce

1 package (8 ounces) shredded mozzarella cheese, divided

12 uncooked whole wheat lasagna noodles

1. Coat inside of **CROCK-POT®** slow cooker with nonstick cooking spray. Heat 1 tablespoon oil in large skillet over medium-high heat. Add onion and salt; cook and stir 5 minutes or until tender. Add garlic; cook and stir 1 minute. Remove to large bowl.

2. Heat 1 tablespoon oil in same skillet. Add zucchini; cook and stir 5 minutes or until lightly browned. Remove mixture to bowl with onion. Repeat with remaining 1 tablespoon oil and squash.

3. Combine ricotta cheese, egg, ¼ cup basil, pepper and ¼ cup Parmesan cheese in medium bowl; stir to blend.

4. Prepare foil handles.* Pour ½ cup marinara sauce evenly into bottom of **CROCK-POT®** slow cooker. Layer 3 lasagna noodles (break to fit evenly); top with ⅔ cup ricotta mixture, ⅓ squash mixture, ¼ cup mozzarella and ½ cup marinara sauce. Repeat layers two times. Top with remaining 3 lasagna noodles, marinara sauce and mozzarella. Sprinkle with remaining ¼ cup Parmesan cheese.

5. Cover; cook on LOW 3 hours. Turn off heat. Uncover; let stand 30 minutes. Sprinkle with remaining 2 tablespoons basil before cutting and serving.

*To make foil handles, tear off three 18X2-inch strips of heavy-duty foil or use regular foil folded to double thickness. Crisscross foil strips in spoke design and place in **CROCK-POT®** slow cooker.

ARTICHOKE PASTA

Makes 4 servings

1 tablespoon olive oil

1 cup chopped sweet onion

4 cloves garlic, minced

1 can (28 ounces) crushed tomatoes

1 can (about 14 ounces) artichoke hearts, drained and cut into pieces

1 cup small pimiento-stuffed olives

¾ teaspoon red pepper flakes

8 ounces hot cooked fettuccine pasta

½ cup grated Asiago or Romano cheese

Fresh basil leaves (optional)

1. Coat inside of **CROCK-POT®** slow cooker with nonstick cooking spray. Heat oil in small skillet over medium heat. Add onion; cook and stir 5 minutes. Add garlic; cook and stir 1 minute. Combine onion mixture, tomatoes, artichokes, olives and red pepper flakes in **CROCK-POT®** slow cooker; stir to blend.

2. Cover; cook on LOW 7 to 8 hours or on HIGH 3 to 4 hours. Top pasta with artichoke sauce and cheese. Garnish with basil.

EGGPLANT ITALIANO

Makes 6 servings

1¼ pounds eggplant, cut into 1-inch cubes

2 onions, thinly sliced

2 stalks celery, cut into 1-inch pieces

1 can (about 14 ounces) diced tomatoes

3 tablespoons tomato sauce

1 tablespoon olive oil

½ cup black olive slices

2 tablespoons balsamic vinegar

1 tablespoon sugar

1 tablespoon capers, drained

1 teaspoon dried oregano or basil

Salt and black pepper

1. Combine eggplant, onions, celery, tomatoes, tomato sauce and oil in **CROCK-POT®** slow cooker; stir to blend. Cover; cook on LOW 3½ to 4 hours.

2. Stir olives, vinegar, sugar, capers and oregano into **CROCK-POT®** slow cooker. Season with salt and pepper. Cover; cook on LOW 45 minutes or until heated through.

THREE-PEPPER PASTA SAUCE

Makes 4 to 6 servings

1 *each* red, yellow and green bell pepper, cut into 1-inch pieces

2 cans (about 14 ounces *each*) diced tomatoes

1 cup chopped onion

1 can (6 ounces) tomato paste

4 cloves garlic, minced

2 tablespoons olive oil

1 teaspoon dried basil

1 teaspoon dried oregano

½ teaspoon salt

¼ teaspoon red pepper flakes or black pepper

Hot cooked pasta

Grated Parmesan or Romano cheese

Combine bell peppers, tomatoes, onion, tomato paste, garlic, oil, basil, oregano, salt and red pepper flakes in **CROCK-POT®** slow cooker; stir to blend. Cover; cook on LOW 7 to 8 hours. Serve with pasta and cheese.

POLENTA LASAGNA

Makes 6 servings

4 cups boiling water

1½ cups whole grain yellow cornmeal

4 teaspoons finely chopped fresh marjoram

1 teaspoon olive oil

1 pound mushrooms, sliced

1 cup chopped leeks

1 clove garlic, minced

½ cup (2 ounces) shredded mozzarella cheese

2 tablespoons chopped fresh basil

1 tablespoon chopped fresh oregano

⅛ teaspoon black pepper

2 medium red bell peppers, chopped

¼ cup water

4 tablespoons freshly grated Parmesan cheese

1. Coat inside of **CROCK-POT®** slow cooker with nonstick cooking spray. Combine 4 cups boiling water and cornmeal in **CROCK-POT®** slow cooker; mix well. Stir in marjoram. Cover; cook on LOW 3 to 4 hours or on HIGH 1 to 2 hours, stirring occasionally. Cover; chill 1 hour or until firm.

2. Heat oil in medium skillet over medium heat. Add mushrooms, leeks and garlic; cook and stir 5 minutes or until leeks are crisp-tender. Stir in mozzarella cheese, basil, oregano and black pepper. Place bell peppers and ¼ cup water in food processor or blender; process until smooth.

3. Cut cold polenta in half and place one half on bottom of **CROCK-POT®** slow cooker. Top with half of bell pepper mixture, half of vegetable mixture and 2 tablespoons Parmesan cheese. Place remaining polenta over Parmesan cheese; layer with remaining bell pepper and vegetable mixtures and Parmesan cheese. Cover; cook on LOW 3 hours or until cheese is melted and polenta is golden brown.

GARDEN PASTA

Makes 4 to 6 servings

1 jar (24 to 26 ounces) puttanesca or spicy tomato basil pasta sauce

1 can (about 14 ounces) stewed tomatoes

1 cup small broccoli florets

½ cup finely diced yellow squash

½ cup finely diced zucchini

½ cup water

2 cups (5 ounces) uncooked bowtie pasta

½ cup crumbled feta cheese

¼ cup chopped fresh basil

1. Coat inside of **CROCK-POT®** slow cooker with nonstick cooking spray. Combine pasta sauce, tomatoes, broccoli, squash, zucchini, water and pasta in **CROCK-POT®** slow cooker; stir to blend.

2. Cover; cook on LOW 3½ to 4½ hours or on HIGH 2 to 2½ hours, stirring halfway through cooking time. Spoon into shallow bowls; top with cheese and basil.

VEGETABLE-BEAN PASTA

Makes 8 servings

2 cans (about 15 ounces *each*) cannellini beans, rinsed and drained

2 cans (about 14 ounces *each*) diced tomatoes

16 baby carrots

1 medium onion, sliced

1 can (6 ounces) tomato paste

1 ounce dried oyster mushrooms, chopped

¼ cup grated Parmesan cheese

2 teaspoons garlic powder

1 teaspoon dried basil

1 teaspoon dried oregano

½ teaspoon dried rosemary

½ teaspoon dried marjoram

½ teaspoon dried sage

½ teaspoon dried thyme

¼ teaspoon black pepper

1 package (12 ounces) whole wheat spaghetti, cooked and drained

1. Combine beans, tomatoes, carrots, onion, tomato paste, mushrooms, cheese, garlic powder, basil, oregano, rosemary, marjoram, sage, thyme and pepper in **CROCK-POT®** slow cooker; stir to blend.

2. Cover; cook on LOW 8 to 10 hours. Serve over spaghetti.

EGGPLANT PARMESAN

Makes 4 servings

¼ cup all-purpose flour

1 teaspoon dried oregano

1 teaspoon dried basil

½ teaspoon salt

1 egg

2 teaspoons cold water

2 tablespoons extra virgin olive oil, divided

1 large eggplant (about 1 pound), ends trimmed, peeled and cut crosswise into 8 slices

2¼ cups spicy marinara pasta sauce

½ cup panko bread crumbs

1½ cups (6 ounces) shredded Italian cheese blend or mozzarella cheese

Chopped fresh basil (optional)

1. Combine flour, oregano, dried basil and salt in shallow dish or pie plate. Beat egg with water in another shallow dish or pie plate.

2. Heat 1 tablespoon oil in large skillet over medium heat. Dip each slice of eggplant in egg mixture, letting excess drip back into dish. Dredge in flour mixture, coating both sides lightly. Cook 4 slices 3 to 4 minutes per side or until lightly browned. Repeat with remaining oil and 4 slices eggplant.

3. Coat inside of **CROCK-POT®** slow cooker with nonstick cooking spray. Layer ¾ cup pasta sauce in bottom of **CROCK-POT®** slow cooker. Arrange 4 slices of browned eggplant over sauce, overlapping if necessary. Top with ¼ cup panko and ½ cup cheese. Repeat layering with ¾ cup pasta sauce, 4 slices eggplant, ¼ cup panko and ½ cup cheese. Spoon remaining pasta sauce over cheese. Cover; cook on LOW 4 to 5 hours or on HIGH 2 to 2½ hours.

4. Sprinkle remaining ½ cup cheese on top. Turn off heat. Let stand, covered, 5 minutes or until cheese is melted. Garnish with fresh basil.

PORTOBELLO BOLOGNESE SAUCE

Makes 4 servings

2 tablespoons extra virgin olive oil

2 cups (6 to 8 ounces) chopped portobello mushrooms

4 cloves garlic, minced

1 jar (24 to 26 ounces) spicy pasta sauce

1 cup thinly sliced carrots

2 tablespoons tomato paste

6 ounces thin spaghetti, uncooked

½ cup grated Parmesan or Romano cheese

¼ cup shredded fresh basil

1. Coat inside of **CROCK-POT®** slow cooker with nonstick cooking spray. Heat oil in large skillet over medium heat. Add mushrooms and garlic; cook 6 minutes or until mushrooms have released their liquid and liquid has thickened slightly.

2. Combine mushroom mixture, pasta sauce, carrots and tomato paste in **CROCK-POT®** slow cooker; mix well. Cover; cook on LOW 5 to 6 hours or on HIGH 2½ to 3 hours or until sauce has thickened and carrots are tender.

3. Cook spaghetti according to package directions. Drain; top with Bolognese sauce, cheese and basil.

CHEESE AND SPINACH LASAGNA

Makes 6 servings

1 container (15 ounces) ricotta cheese

1 package (10 ounces) frozen chopped spinach, thawed and squeezed dry

2 cups (8 ounces) shredded mozzarella cheese, divided

1 egg

½ cup grated Parmesan cheese, divided

1 jar (24 to 26 ounces) pasta sauce

½ cup water

6 uncooked lasagna noodles

1. Combine ricotta cheese, spinach, 1½ cups mozzarella cheese, egg and ¼ cup Parmesan cheese in large bowl; mix well.

2. Mix pasta sauce and water in another large bowl. Spoon 1 cup of sauce mixture into **CROCK-POT®** slow cooker coated with nonstick cooking spray. Layer 2 noodles over sauce (breaking to fit). Spoon ½ cup sauce mixture over noodles. Spoon half of ricotta mixture over pasta sauce. Add 2 more noodles and remaining ricotta mixture. Top with remaining 2 noodles and remaining pasta sauce.

3. Cover; cook on LOW 4 to 6 hours or until liquid is absorbed and noodles are tender. Sprinkle remaining ½ cup mozzarella cheese and ¼ cup Parmesan cheese over top; cover and let stand 5 minutes or until cheese is melted.

SIDES & MORE

ITALIAN EGGPLANT WITH MILLET AND PEPPER STUFFING

Makes 4 servings

¼ cup uncooked millet

2 small eggplants (about ¾ pound *total*), unpeeled

¼ cup chopped red bell pepper, divided

¼ cup chopped green bell pepper, divided

1 teaspoon olive oil

1 clove garlic, minced

1½ cups vegetable broth

½ teaspoon ground cumin

½ teaspoon dried oregano

⅛ teaspoon red pepper flakes

Sprigs fresh basil (optional)

1. Heat large skillet over medium heat. Add millet; cook and stir 5 minutes. Remove to small bowl; set aside. Cut eggplants lengthwise into halves. Scoop out flesh, leaving about ¼-inch-thick shell. Reserve shells; chop eggplant flesh. Combine 1 tablespoon red bell pepper and 1 tablespoon green bell pepper in small bowl; set aside.

2. Heat oil in same skillet over medium heat. Add chopped eggplant, remaining red and green bell peppers and garlic; cook and stir 8 minutes or until eggplant is tender.

3. Combine eggplant mixture, broth, cumin, oregano and red pepper flakes in **CROCK-POT®** slow cooker. Cover; cook on LOW 4½ hours or until all liquid is absorbed.

4. Turn **CROCK-POT®** slow cooker to HIGH. Fill eggplant shells with eggplant-millet mixture. Sprinkle with reserved bell peppers. Place filled shells in **CROCK-POT®** slow cooker. Cover; cook on HIGH 1½ to 2 hours. Garnish with basil.

RISI BISI

Makes 6 servings

1½ cups uncooked converted long grain rice

¾ cup chopped onion

2 cloves garlic, minced

2 cans (about 14 ounces *each*) vegetable broth

⅓ cup water

¾ teaspoon Italian seasoning

½ teaspoon dried basil

½ cup frozen peas, thawed

¼ cup grated Parmesan cheese

¼ cup toasted pine nuts (optional)*

To toast nuts, spread in single layer in heavy skillet. Cook and stir over medium heat 1 to 2 minutes or until nuts are lightly browned.

1. Combine rice, onion and garlic in **CROCK-POT®** slow cooker.

2. Bring broth and water to a boil in small saucepan. Stir broth mixture, Italian seasoning and basil into rice mixture in **CROCK-POT®** slow cooker. Cover; cook on LOW 2 to 3 hours or until liquid is absorbed.

3. Add peas to **CROCK-POT®** slow cooker. Cover; cook on LOW 1 hour. Stir in cheese. Garnish with pine nuts.

PARMESAN POTATO WEDGES

Makes 6 servings

2 pounds red potatoes, cut into
½-inch wedges

¼ cup finely chopped yellow onion

1½ teaspoons dried oregano

½ teaspoon salt

¼ teaspoon black pepper

2 tablespoons butter, cubed

¼ cup grated Parmesan cheese

Layer potatoes, onion, oregano, salt and pepper in **CROCK-POT®** slow cooker; dot with butter. Cover; cook on HIGH 4 hours. Remove potatoes to large serving platter; sprinkle with cheese.

ASIAGO AND ASPARAGUS RISOTTO-STYLE RICE

Makes 4 servings

2 cups chopped onion

1 can (about 14 ounces) vegetable broth

1 cup uncooked converted rice

2 cloves garlic, minced

½ pound asparagus spears, trimmed and broken into 1-inch pieces

1 cup half-and-half, divided

½ cup (about 4 ounces) grated Asiago cheese, plus additional for garnish

¼ cup (½ stick) butter, cubed

½ cup (2 ounces) pine nuts or slivered almonds, toasted*

1 teaspoon salt

To toast nuts, spread in single layer in heavy skillet. Cook and stir over medium heat 1 to 2 minutes or until nuts are lightly browned.

1. Place onion, broth, rice and garlic into **CROCK-POT®** slow cooker; stir until well blended. Cover; cook on HIGH 2 hours or until rice is tender.

2. Stir in asparagus and ½ cup half-and-half. Cover; cook on HIGH 20 minutes or until asparagus is crisp-tender.

3. Stir in remaining ½ cup half-and-half, ½ cup cheese, butter, pine nuts and salt. Turn off heat. Cover; let stand 5 minutes or until cheese is slightly melted. Fluff with fork. Garnish with additional cheese.

TIP: Risotto is a classic creamy rice dish of Northern Italy and can be made with a wide variety of ingredients. Fresh vegetables and cheeses such as Asiago work especially well in risotto. Parmesan cheese, shellfish, white wine and herbs are also popular additions.

FENNEL BRAISED WITH TOMATO

Makes 6 servings

1 tablespoon olive oil

2 fennel bulbs, quartered, cored, thinly sliced, tops removed and fronds reserved for garnish

1 onion, sliced

1 clove garlic, sliced

4 tomatoes, chopped

⅔ cup vegetable broth

3 tablespoons dry white wine

1 tablespoon chopped fresh marjoram *or* 1 teaspoon dried marjoram

Salt and black pepper

1. Heat oil in large skillet over medium heat. Add fennel bulbs, onion and garlic; cook and stir 5 minutes or until onion is soft and translucent. Remove fennel mixture to **CROCK-POT®** slow cooker. Add tomatoes, broth, wine, marjoram, salt and pepper; stir to blend.

2. Cover; cook on LOW 2 to 3 hours or on HIGH 1 to 1½ hours. Garnish with fennel fronds.

PESTO RICE AND BEANS

Makes 8 servings

1 can (about 15 ounces) Great Northern beans, rinsed and drained

1 can (about 14 ounces) vegetable broth

¾ cup uncooked converted long grain rice

1½ cups frozen cut green beans, thawed and drained

½ cup prepared pesto

Grated Parmesan cheese (optional)

1. Combine Great Northern beans, broth and rice in **CROCK-POT®** slow cooker. Cover; cook on LOW 2 hours.

2. Stir in green beans. Cover; cook on LOW 1 hour or until rice and beans are tender.

3. Turn off heat. Remove **CROCK-POT®** slow cooker stoneware to heatproof surface. Stir in pesto and cheese, if desired. Let stand, covered, 5 minutes or until cheese is melted. Serve immediately.

WHITE BEANS AND TOMATOES

Makes 8 to 10 servings

¼ cup olive oil

2 medium onions, chopped

1 tablespoon minced garlic

4 cups water

2 cans (about 14 ounces *each*) cannellini beans, rinsed and drained

1 can (about 28 ounces) crushed tomatoes

4 teaspoons dried oregano

2 teaspoons kosher salt

Black pepper (optional)

Sprigs fresh oregano (optional)

1. Heat oil in large skillet over medium heat. Add onions; cook 15 minutes or until tender and translucent, stirring occasionally. Add garlic; cook 1 minute.

2. Remove mixture to **CROCK-POT®** slow cooker. Add water, beans, tomatoes, dried oregano and salt. Cover; cook on LOW 8 hours or on HIGH 4 hours. Stir in pepper, if desired. Garnish with fresh oregano.

CHEESY POLENTA

Makes 6 servings

6 cups vegetable broth

1½ cups uncooked medium-grind instant polenta

½ cup grated Parmesan cheese, plus additional for serving

4 tablespoons (½ stick) unsalted butter, cubed

Fried sage leaves (optional)

1. Coat inside of **CROCK-POT®** slow cooker with nonstick cooking spray. Heat broth in large saucepan over high heat. Remove to **CROCK-POT®** slow cooker; whisk in polenta.

2. Cover; cook on LOW 2 to 2½ hours or until polenta is tender and creamy. Stir in ½ cup cheese and butter. Serve with additional cheese. Garnish with sage.

TIP: Spread any leftover polenta in a baking dish and refrigerate until cold. Cut cold polenta into sticks or slices. You can then fry or grill the polenta until lightly browned.

LEMON-MINT RED POTATOES

Makes 4 servings

2 pounds new red potatoes

3 tablespoons extra virgin olive oil

1 teaspoon salt

½ teaspoon Greek seasoning or dried oregano

¼ teaspoon garlic powder

¼ teaspoon black pepper

4 tablespoons chopped fresh mint, divided

2 tablespoons butter

2 tablespoons lemon juice

1 teaspoon grated lemon peel

1. Coat inside of **CROCK-POT®** slow cooker with nonstick cooking spray. Add potatoes and oil, stirring gently to coat. Sprinkle with salt, Greek seasoning, garlic powder and pepper. Cover; cook on LOW 7 hours or on HIGH 4 hours.

2. Stir in 2 tablespoons mint, butter, lemon juice and lemon peel until butter is completely melted. Cover; cook on HIGH 15 minutes. Sprinkle with remaining 2 tablespoons mint.

TIP: It's easy to prepare these potatoes ahead of time. Simply follow the recipe and then turn off the heat. Let it stand at room temperature for up to 2 hours. You may reheat or serve the potatoes at room temperature.

SPINACH RISOTTO

Makes 4 servings

2 teaspoons butter

2 teaspoons olive oil

3 tablespoons finely chopped shallot

1¼ cups uncooked Arborio rice

½ cup dry white wine

3 cups chicken broth

½ teaspoon salt

2 cups baby spinach

¼ cup grated Parmesan cheese

2 tablespoons pine nuts, toasted*

*To toast pine nuts, spread in single layer in heavy skillet. Cook and stir over medium heat 1 to 2 minutes or until nuts are lightly browned.

1. Melt butter in medium skillet over medium heat; add oil. Add shallot; cook and stir until softened but not browned.

2. Stir in rice; cook 2 minutes or until well coated. Stir in wine; cook until reduced by half. Remove to **CROCK-POT®** slow cooker. Stir broth and salt into **CROCK-POT®** slow cooker. Cover; cook on HIGH 2 to 2½ hours or until rice is almost cooked but still contains a little liquid.

3. Stir in spinach. Cover; cook on HIGH 15 to 20 minutes or until rice is tender and creamy. Gently stir in cheese and pine nuts just before serving.

FRESH BOSC PEAR GRANITA

Makes 6 servings

1 pound fresh Bosc pears, peeled, cored and cubed

1¼ cups water

¼ cup sugar

½ teaspoon ground cinnamon

1 tablespoon lemon juice

Fresh raspberries (optional)

Lemon slices (optional)

Fresh mint leaves (optional)

1. Place pears, water, sugar and cinnamon in **CROCK-POT®** slow cooker. Cover; cook on HIGH 2½ to 3½ hours or until pears are very soft and tender. Stir in lemon juice.

2. Remove pears and syrup to blender or food processor; blend until smooth. Strain mixture, discarding any pulp. Pour liquid into 13×9-inch baking pan. Cover tightly with plastic wrap. Place pan in freezer.

3. Stir every hour, tossing granita with fork. Crush any lumps in mixture as it freezes. Freeze 3 to 4 hours or until firm. You may keep granita in freezer up to 2 days before serving; toss granita every 6 to 12 hours. Garnish with raspberries, lemon slices and mint.

ITALIAN CHEESECAKE

Makes 16 servings

- 6 graham crackers, crushed to fine crumbs
- 2 tablespoons packed brown sugar
- 2 tablespoons unsalted butter, melted
- 2 packages (8 ounces *each*) cream cheese
- 1½ cups granulated sugar
- 1 container (15 ounces) ricotta cheese

- 2 cups sour cream
- 1 teaspoon vanilla
- 4 eggs
- 3 tablespoons all-purpose flour
- 3 tablespoons cornstarch
- 3 graham crackers, broken into 1-inch pieces (optional)
- Fresh strawberries (optional)
- Fresh mint (optional)

1. Prepare foil handles by tearing off three 18×2-inch strips heavy foil (or use regular foil folded to double thickness). Crisscross foil strips in spoke design; place in **CROCK-POT®** slow cooker. Coat inside of 5-quart **CROCK-POT®** slow cooker with nonstick cooking spray.

2. Combine crushed graham crackers and brown sugar in medium bowl. Stir in melted butter until crumbs hold shape when pinched. Pat firmly into **CROCK-POT®** slow cooker. Refrigerate until needed.

3. Beat cream cheese and granulated sugar in large bowl with electric mixer at medium speed until smooth. Add ricotta, sour cream and vanilla; beat until blended. Add eggs, one at a time, beating well after each addition. Beat in flour and cornstarch. Pour filling into prepared crust. Cover; cook on LOW 3 to 4 hours or until cheesecake is nearly set.

4. Turn off heat. Remove lid; cover top of stoneware with clean kitchen towel. Replace lid; cool 1 hour. Remove stoneware from base; cool completely. Remove cheesecake to serving plate using foil handles. Cover; refrigerate until serving. Garnish with graham cracker pieces, strawberries and mint.

INDEX

Italian Eggplant with Millet and Pepper Stuffing (page 163)

Chicken Vesuvio (page 80)

METRIC CONVERSION CHART

VOLUME MEASUREMENTS (dry)

$^1\!/_8$ teaspoon = 0.5 mL
$^1\!/_4$ teaspoon = 1 mL
$^1\!/_2$ teaspoon = 2 mL
$^3\!/_4$ teaspoon = 4 mL
1 teaspoon = 5 mL
1 tablespoon = 15 mL
2 tablespoons = 30 mL
$^1\!/_4$ cup = 60 mL
$^1\!/_3$ cup = 75 mL
$^1\!/_2$ cup = 125 mL
$^2\!/_3$ cup = 150 mL
$^3\!/_4$ cup = 175 mL
1 cup = 250 mL
2 cups = 1 pint = 500 mL
3 cups = 750 mL
4 cups = 1 quart = 1 L

VOLUME MEASUREMENTS (fluid)

1 fluid ounce (2 tablespoons) = 30 mL
4 fluid ounces ($^1\!/_2$ cup) = 125 mL
8 fluid ounces (1 cup) = 250 mL
12 fluid ounces (1$^1\!/_2$ cups) = 375 mL
16 fluid ounces (2 cups) = 500 mL

WEIGHTS (mass)

$^1\!/_2$ ounce = 15 g
1 ounce = 30 g
3 ounces = 90 g
4 ounces = 120 g
8 ounces = 225 g
10 ounces = 285 g
12 ounces = 360 g
16 ounces = 1 pound = 450 g

DIMENSIONS

$^1\!/_{16}$ inch = 2 mm
$^1\!/_8$ inch = 3 mm
$^1\!/_4$ inch = 6 mm
$^1\!/_2$ inch = 1.5 cm
$^3\!/_4$ inch = 2 cm
1 inch = 2.5 cm

OVEN TEMPERATURES

250°F = 120°C
275°F = 140°C
300°F = 150°C
325°F = 160°C
350°F = 180°C
375°F = 190°C
400°F = 200°C
425°F = 220°C
450°F = 230°C

BAKING PAN SIZES

Utensil	Size in Inches/Quarts	Metric Volume	Size in Centimeters
Baking or Cake Pan (square or rectangular)	8×8×2	2 L	20×20×5
	9×9×2	2.5 L	23×23×5
	12×8×2	3 L	30×20×5
	13×9×2	3.5 L	33×23×5
Loaf Pan	8×4×3	1.5 L	20×10×7
	9×5×3	2 L	23×13×7
Round Layer Cake Pan	8×1½	1.2 L	20×4
	9×1½	1.5 L	23×4
Pie Plate	8×1¼	750 mL	20×3
	9×1¼	1 L	23×3
Baking Dish or Casserole	1 quart	1 L	—
	1½ quart	1.5 L	—
	2 quart	2 L	—